THE
*LITURGICAL
MINISTRY
SERIES*

GUIDE FOR DEACONS

Bob Puhala
Paul Turner

LTP

LITURGY
TRAINING
PUBLICATIONS

Nihil Obstat
Very Reverend Daniel A. Smilanic, JCD
Vicar for Canonical Services
Archdiocese of Chicago
August 8, 2011

Imprimatur
Reverend Monsignor John F. Canary, STL, DMIN
Vicar General
Archdiocese of Chicago
August 8, 2011

THE LITURGICAL MINISTRY SERIES: GUIDE FOR DEACONS © 2011 Archdiocese of Chicago: Liturgy Training Publications, 3949 South Racine Avenue, Chicago IL 60609; 1-800-933-1800, fax 1-800-933-7094, e-mail orders@ltp.org. All rights reserved. See our Web site at www.LTP.org.

Photos © John Zich

Printed in the United States of America.

Library of Congress Control Number: 2011931440

ISBN 978-1-61671-046-0

ELDEA

Psalm 117

Praise the LORD, all you nations!
    Extol him, all you peoples!
For great is his steadfast love toward us,
    and the faithfulness of the
    LORD endures forever.
Praise the LORD!

Table of Contents

Preface

They chose Stephen, a man full of faith and the Holy Spirit, together with Philip, Prochorus, Nicanor, Timon, Parmenas, and Nicholas, a proselyte of Antioch. They had these men stand before the apostles, who prayed and laid their hands on them.

—*Acts 6:5–6*

Chicken sales were down, and Timon was not happy. Even his business partner Nicanor was unable to lift his spirits. "God will take care of us, Timon. People need chickens. When money is scarce, chickens don't sell. But eventually they will. Everyone needs chickens."

"I have to feed my wife and kids," Timon mused. "I can't wait forever." After he became a Christian, Timon's immediate family seemed more loving and happier. But their new faith came at a cost. Some members of his extended family were not happy. They preferred the religion of their ancestors. His cousin had practically spit on him when he said, "Your chickens won't sell because the gods are displeased." Timon could not believe it.

Just then a shout reached his ears. "Timon! Nicanor!" The chickens cackled and shook their fathers. Nicanor raised his head. "Epaphras! Mary! What's going on?"

"Come with us! Hurry up! We need you." Mary was breathless, but her face beamed with excitement. "We need you now."

"Calm down," said Timon. "We can't go anywhere right now. We have to sell chickens."

"No, really. It can't wait," said Epaphras. "Peter, James, John—all of the Twelve just had a meeting. They need help. They need you."

"I still don't get it. What happened?" asked Nicanor.

"There's been a dispute," said Epaphras.

Mary nodded. "Between Hebrew Christians like my family and Greek Christians like his," she said, pointing to Epaphras.

"My family said Mary's family was getting more food than they were," said Epaphras. "It got nasty," said Mary.

Nicanor and Timon stared in disbelief. There had always been a little unrest between the groups who were becoming Christians, but in the past they somehow managed to set their disagreements aside.

Timon the businessman wanted the facts. "Is it true? Were Hebrew Christians cheating Greek Christians?"

Epaphras said, "The Twelve wouldn't say. At first they just dodged the whole issue. It made my family think that the Twelve were guilty as charged."

"So they came up with another idea," said Mary.

"We thought they were just trying to wiggle out of trouble," said Epaphras, "but the more we heard them speak, the better the idea sounded."

Now Nicanor was getting excited. "What is it? What did they decide to do?"

Mary said, "They finally admitted they need help. They cannot go on this way—leading the community in prayer, preaching the word of God to strangers, baptizing new converts, and feeding the entire community all by themselves. They need help."

Nicanor and Timon looked at each other. They could tell where this was leading.

"So, what do they want?" asked Timon.

Epaphras said, "They want help with the tables."[1]

"With the tables?" Nicanor exclaimed, a little taken aback. He loved the other Christians, and he honestly felt ready to die for Christ if it ever came to that. But he thought he had more skills than the Twelve were recognizing. "Tables," he said, imagining himself distributing food carefully to make sure everybody got just what they needed, handling the complaints, and then straighten things up when everyone had been fed. He wanted to share his faith—not clean up after it.

Timon asked, "So what's the emergency? Why do they need us now?"

Epaphras sprang the trap. "They asked us to find seven men with a good reputation, men filled with the Holy Spirit and wisdom, men who would perform tasks great or small for the sake of the kingdom of God." Timon raised his hands to protest. "There's more," continued Epaphras. "They will pray over these men."

"What?" asked Nicanor, finally realizing that this was going to mean more than kitchen detail.

"That's right. They want to impose hands on the seven of them, pray that they will receive the Holy Spirit, and appoint them formally to this task. They want leaders," said Epaphras.

"We talked it over," said Mary, "and we quickly assembled our list of seven men." She smiled. "Everyone agrees. We want you. We want you both."

Nicanor couldn't believe his ears. He could see the issues. It wasn't just about counting loaves of bread. It was about easing pain, building community, strengthening faith, and offering thanks to God. He needed no more convincing.

"Let's go!" said Timon. He and Nicanor embraced each other and started off with Epaphras and Mary.

"Hey! Hey!" a voice behind them called. "I need chickens. Are you selling chickens?" Timon looked back. He had left the chickens behind. He looked at Epaphras and at Mary's pleading face. Then he looked at the buyer, a smartly dressed man ready to rescue his tottering business.

"Take them," Timon said. "Just take the chickens." He followed Nicanor up the road.

Paul Turner

NOTES

1. See Acts 6:1–6.

Welcome

Deacons proclaim the Gospel of Jesus Christ in three primary ways. They assist during the liturgy. They serve the needy in the community. They preach.

Many deacons are single men who are preparing for their ordination to the priesthood. Their diaconate serves as an internship for the joys and demands of priesthood. We call them transitional deacons because they serve the Church as deacons during an interim period of their life.

Other deacons commit to this ministry as a lifelong service. We call them permanent deacons. They spend their years of preparation to serve as deacons specifically serve. Some of them are single, yet they have not felt the call to priesthood. Most of them are married. As baptized and confirmed members of the community, they have already accepted the responsibility to bear witness to the faith they profess. As married members of the community, they demonstrate the holiness of wedded love. As ordained members of the community, they possess the special charisms of deacons. Their entire lives bear witness to the interplay between faith and service, between worship and charity. Their lives enrich the Church.

Whether you are a transitional or a permanent deacon, you are a deacon. You are ordained for service. Congratulations to you on hearing and pursuing your vocation. The Church needs you and thanks you for answering God's call.

About This Book

This book will offer you some guidance to assist your ministry. You will learn about the history of the diaconate and how the Church understands your role. You will find some reflections to help develop your spirituality, whether you are single or married. This book will give you practical advice on many aspects of the liturgical service you offer the Church. And it will answer the most frequently asked questions about diaconal ministry. At the end there will be a selection of resources for further reading, as well as a helpful glossary.

As you serve the Church in this ministry, may you find your life enriched. May you experience the joy in hearing the call of the people of God, and in responding to the voice of Christ.

About the Authors

This book has been written by two authors. PAUL TURNER wrote the first sections of the book, "Preface," "Welcome," "Theology and History of the Deacon," and "Spirituality and Formation of the Deacon." He is the pastor of St. Munchin parish in Cameron, Missouri, and its mission, St. Aloysius in Maysville. A priest of the diocese of Kansas City–St. Joseph, he holds a doctorate in sacred theology from Sant' Anselmo in Rome. He is the author of many pastoral resources about sacraments and the liturgy. BOB PUHALA is director of the Deacon Formation Program at the University of St. Mary of the Lake/Mundelein Seminary for the Archdiocese of Chicago. He was ordained a deacon in 1998. Puhala is also a member of the Board of Directors for the National Association of Diaconate Directors. Holding an MSJ from the Medill School of Journalism, Puhala has written more than 30 travel/general interest books. He is married, with two daughters, and lives in the Chicago area.

Questions for Discussion and Reflection

1. Why have you agreed to serve as a deacon in the Church?

    _____

    _____

2. What do you hope to gain in your understanding of the theology and function of the ministry through this book?

    _____

    _____

Theology and History of the Deacon

The Son of Man came not to be served but to serve.
—*Matthew 20:28*

Historical Roots

The origin of the diaconate is described in Acts 6:1–6. If all you knew about deacons was restricted to those verses, you would conclude that the purpose of deacons is the orderly distribution of food to members of the community. Deacons, however, do much more and have since the earliest days of the Church. Within a few short chapters of Acts, deacons are preaching the Gospel, baptizing new converts, and even losing their lives in the first persecution of Christians.

It is difficult to pin down exactly what the first deacons were expected to do. Without question, they were people of great faith who accepted responsibilities of leadership in the community. The Church expected exemplary behavior from deacons. When reading about deacons of the past, we should not import too much of what we know of deacons in the present.

The New Testament

The New Testament was written in Greek, and the word it uses most often for the kind of service all Christians give is *diakonia*. From that we get our word "deacon." This may be why Luke situated the origin of deacons in a story about waiting tables. Anybody could wait tables. But the task at hand needed leaders with a strong faith, a sense of justice, a desire for charity, and well-respected personal qualities. Even with all these qualifications, deacons had to be willing to get their hands dirty, to perform menial tasks for the community. As the role of deacon evolved, it never lost its firm original vision. The diaconate was never about glamour; it concerned service.

In the Gospel accounts, some of the ordinary service performed by women was called *diakonia*. After Jesus healed Peter's mother-in-law in the presence of several followers, she served them.[1] Many women followed Jesus to serve him in his ministry.[2] When Jesus visited their home, Martha asked him to have Mary help with the serving.[3] In all these instances, the Greek word used in the New Testament to describe service is the one that Christians later adopted for deacons.

Jesus used the same word in many of his sayings. He came not to be served, but to serve.[4] He came not to sit at a table, but as one who serves.[5] The first must be last and the servant of all.[6] He modeled this kind of service when he washed feet at the Last Supper and urged his disciples to do the same.[7] Jesus apparently felt that all his followers should give *diakonia*—a humble service of others, taken up freely, which in turn would win the respect of others.

Saint Paul used the same word. He acknowledged the variety of services (*diakonion*) in the Christian community,[8] the gifts that allow service to happen.[9] He described himself as a servant (*diakonos*).[10] He was probably referring to his work as an evangelizer. But in one passage he used *diakonon* for his ministry of carrying contributions to the poor in Jerusalem.[11] Paul never explicitly used *diakonos* in reference to a minister at worship. He spoke of the service of one leader named Stephanas,[12] and called one woman, Phoebe, a *diakonos*.[13] He acknowledged the work of other *diakonoi* named Epaphras and Tychicus.[14]

> *Deacons likewise must be serious, not double-tongued, not indulging in much wine, not greedy for money; they must hold fast to the mystery of the faith with a clear conscience.*
>
> —*1 Timothy 3:8*

Perhaps the most tantalizing Pauline verse concerning deacons is the opening of the letter to the Philippians. This is thought to be an early letter of Paul, one written to a community that he had personally helped establish. He sent the letter to all the members of the community at Philippi, but especially to the Bishops and deacons. This is probably the first reference to deacons in the entire New Testament because the letters of Paul predate the Acts of the Apostles. Already there were people known as deacons or servants, who shared leadership together with the Bishops or overseers.

This link between Bishops and deacons became all the more explicit in the pastoral epistles,[15] considered to be among the late writings of the New Testament. They describe a more institutionalized and hierarchical Church. The most famous passage from these is in 1 Timothy. After presenting what is expected of Bishops, the writer makes these points about deacons:

> Deacons likewise must be serious, not double-tongued, not indulging in much wine, not greedy for money; they must hold fast to the mystery of the faith with a clear conscience. And let them first be tested; then, if they prove themselves blameless, let them serve as deacons. Women likewise must be serious, not slanderers, but temperate, faithful in all things. Let deacons be married only once, and let them manage their children and their households well; for those who serve well as deacons gain a good standing for themselves and great boldness in the faith that is in Christ Jesus.[16]

As the letter to the Philippians opened with the pairing of Bishops and deacons, so this passage contains an elaborate list of expectations of the two kinds of leaders. Deacons had to lead communities, but they would only be effective if they were persons of character. The Acts of the Apostles concurs with this when it describes the qualities required of the first deacons. The absence of any reference to a role at the liturgy is noteworthy.

In the middle of this passage from 1 Timothy is a line about women. This instruction may concern wives of deacons, or else women who served as deacons, such as Phoebe.

Timothy himself is asked to carry on the work of an evangelist, which is the work of his *diakonia*.[17] Turning back to the Acts of the Apostles, it is easy to see why. What began as table service, quickly matured into evangelization. The preaching of Barnabas and Saul is called their *diakonia*.[18] Philip the deacon, whose ministry of preaching and baptizing begins early in his career,[19] is later called an evangelist.[20]

The most famous of all the New Testament deacons is Stephen. He is the first of the seven to be listed in Acts 6, where he alone is singled out as a man of faith and the Holy Spirit.[21] The story immediately turns to focus on his ministry of preaching, teaching, and working miracles.[22] Seen as a threat to authority, Stephen was arrested and put on trial, where there are many parallels to the end of his life and the Passion of Jesus Christ.[23] Stoned to death, he became the first martyr of the young Christian community, a people who remembered him with great admiration.

Deacons in the New Testament were called by a name that meant "servant." They served in leadership roles for communities. They preached. They tended the needs of the poor. They were of exceptional character. In time, their example would carry the word "deacon" forward to a more specialized role within the Church.

The Early Church

In the post-apostolic Church, certain ministers continued to be identified as deacons. Around the end of the first century, a letter attributed to Clement of Rome was sent to the Church at Corinth. Probably referring to the evidence in the letters of Paul, the author states that the apostles tested certain members of the community for their spirituality, and then appointed them as Bishops and deacons so that they could serve the increasing numbers of believers.[24] This same letter distinguished the functions of certain ministers called the high priest, the priests and the "Levites"—probably a reference to Bishops, priests, and deacons. It began an association of Christian deacons with Old Testament Levites,[25] a comparison that became important in ordination prayers many centuries later.

Around the same time, Ignatius of Antioch, on his way to martyrdom, wrote inspirational letters to six churches and one saint (Polycarp). He mentions these three ranks of ministers: Bishops, presbyters, and deacons. He calls Bishops those who preside over the community, presbyters those who act like the apostles, and deacons those who share in the ministry of Jesus Christ.[26] The presbyters and deacons were united with one Bishop. They were part of one Church, and their unity fostered that of those who share Eucharist.[27] Deacons performed the ministry of Jesus Christ, and Ignatius expects them to serve only after winning the approval of the community. He requires them to be leaders of outstanding character because they are not just ministers of food and drink, but of the Church of God.[28]

In the second century, Polycarp stressed that deacons are servants of God and Christ, not of people, and that they need to be individuals of good character. He called on young people to obey the deacons of the Church.[29]

It did not always work out the way it was intended. In the middle of the third century, Cyprian of Carthage responded to a Bishop complaining that his own deacon had insulted him. Cyprian advised his colleague to put the deacon in his place.[30] He notes in the same passage that Bishops appoint deacons. In another letter he states that he consults the clergy and the people before any ordination.[31]

The *Apostolic Tradition* hands down rites for ordinations from the third to fourth century. It requests that deacons be chosen for their good qualities, and that the Bishop alone impose hands on them. Deacons were ordained for service to the Bishop, not for priests.[32] They reported to the Bishop each day to receive a work assignment,[33] often visiting the sick on his behalf.[34] The deacon exercised administrative responsibilities for the Bishop. During Baptisms, deacons enter the water with catechumens, where they elicit a profession of faith.[35] At Eucharist they brought the bread and wine to the Bishop.[36]

Still, the Council of Nicaea faced a situation in which some deacons were presuming more authority than they had. They were giving Holy Communion to priests. The council stated that deacons were ministers of the Bishop and subordinate to presbyters. They were to receive Holy Communion from a Bishop or a presbyter. These concerns may have signaled a sea change in the work of deacons. Some of them apparently had taken their administrative responsibilities too far. Now their authority was being restricted, and their liturgical role was starting to crystallize.

Around the same time, Eusebius quoted a letter from Cornelius detailing the number of ministers present in Rome. The deacons numbered seven, which probably remained a fixed number in imitation of the first deacons in Acts 6.[37]

Jerome (+420) elaborated the imagery from the *Letter of Clement,* stating that the Bishop, priests and deacons occupy the same positions in the Church as Aaron, his sons and the Levites.[38] Jerome was objecting to deacons who had taken on too much authority. In Rome, for example, the seven deacons were appointing priests.

Problematic deacons so disturbed Gregory the Great that the first decree of his synod in the year 595 was directed against them.[39] Apparently some skilled singers had managed to be ordained deacons.

They sang beautifully at the liturgy—too beautifully. Gregory feared that they were singing for people, not for God, and by focusing on their musical ministry, they neglected their duties as preachers and caregivers for the poor. He forbade them to sing anything except to chant the Gospel. Today it is hoped that deacons will be singers, but in those days singers were becoming deacons. In Gregory's time, the liturgical function of deacons was alluring to some men, but the role still carried other expectations for the spread of the Gospel and the care of the needy.

Deacons in the Middle Ages

By the seventh century, the deacon's responsibilities refocused on the liturgy. Isidore of Seville summed up a deacon's duties in this way: they assisted priests, helped with Baptisms and anointings, the handling of sacred vessels, bringing and arranging the offerings on the altar, carrying the cross, proclaiming the readings from the New Testament, offering prayers, and announcing the exchange of peace.[40]

The ordination ceremony for deacons went through an elaborate development during the Middle Ages. It was then customary for the clergy and the people to select those to be ordained. Pope Leo the Great promoted ordinations on Sundays. But Pope Gelasius preferred Saturday ordinations on the ember days of early Lent, June, September, and December.[41]

After the prayer of ordination, only one Bishop imposed hands to ordain a deacon, as envisioned in the *Apostolic Tradition*.[42] (Other clergy imposed hands to ordain a priest.) A deacon was being ordained for the Bishop, not to join the ranks of priests, nor to form a federation of deacons. During the ceremony he put on special vestments and was given the kiss of peace.

The blessing for deacons in the *Verona Sacramentary* prayed that they might fulfill their holy ministry at the altar.[43] It called the diaconate a Levitical ministry. Just as Christian priesthood fulfilled the Old Testament priesthood, so did the diaconate fulfill the ministry of the Levites, who assisted the Old Testament priests.[44]

By the eighth century the *Gelasian Sacramentary*'s prayer for blessing deacons aligned their ministry to that of angels, who ministered to Jesus at the time of his sacrifice and Resurrection.[45] It also referred back to the seven deacons whom the Apostles chose under the guidance of the Holy Spirit.[46]

In the tenth century the rites of ordination in the Roman-Germanic Pontifical had collected evolving practices from different parts of the Catholic world. They included a blessing for the vestments and a text for putting on the stole: "Receive your stole, fulfill your ministry, for God has the power to increase his grace in you."[47] The deacon was also presented with the *Book of the Gospels* with these words: "Receive the power of reading the gospel in the church of God both for the living and for the dead, in the name of the Lord."[48]

The sixteenth-century Council of Trent considered the restoration of the diaconate as an independent order within the Church, but "it was much later that the idea matured."[49]

The liturgical functions of deacons matured in the Missal of 1570, which went virtually unchanged for 400 years. Among the deacon's duties were to assist with the incense, to recite the Gloria with the priest, to proclaim the Gospel, to pour water in the chalice at the offertory, to recite the *Confiteor* before Holy Communion, and to give the dismissal. During the Easter Vigil, the deacon sang the *Exsultet*, the proclamation of the Resurrection of Christ.

Deacons and the Post-Conciliar Church: A Theology of Service

This liturgical role solidified the primary image of deacons for many hundreds of years. Throughout the twentieth century a new impetus sought to expand the deacon's role. Whereas a deacon had performed a purely liturgical function during the brief time before he was ordained a priest, advocates sought to recognize the diaconate as a vocation unto itself. In 1947, Pope Pius XII settled a question about the status of deacons when he affirmed that they receive the sacrament of Holy Orders with by imposition of hands.[50] This elevated the conversation about the diaconate.

In time, the Second Vatican Council (1962–1965) issued its *Dogmatic Constitution on the Church* (*Lumen Gentium*), which called for the restoration of the diaconal ministry as a permanent way of life.

> For, strengthened by sacramental grace, [deacons] . . . are dedicated to the people of God, in communion with the bishop and his presbyterate, in the service of the liturgy, of the word and of charity. It is a deacon's task, as authorized by the competent authority, to administer Baptism solemnly, to reserve and distribute the Eucharist, to assist at and to bless marriages in the name of the church, to take Viaticum to the dying, to read the sacred scripture to the faithful, to instruct and exhort the people, to preside over the worship and the prayer of the faithful, to administer sacramentals, and to officiate at funeral and burial services.[51]

This opinion was corroborated in the *Decree on the Mission Activity of the Church* (*Ad gentes*).

> Wherever it appears opportune to episcopal conferences, the diaconate should be restored as a permanent state of life, in accordance with the norms of the constitution on the church (See Vatican Council II, Dogmatic Constitution on the Church, *Lumen gentium*, 29). It would help those men who carry out the ministry of the diaconate—preaching the word of God as catechists, governing scattered christian communities in the name of the bishop or parish priest, or exercising charity in the performances of social or charitable works— if they were to be strengthened by the imposition of hands which has come down from the apostles. They would be more closely bound to the altar and their ministry would be made more fruitful through the sacramental grace of the diaconate.[52]

After the Council, Pope Paul VI restored the diaconate to its own independent rank by his *motu proprio, Sacrum diaconatus ordinem*.[53] Since then, the number of permanent deacons has grown. Their mission does not differ from those of transitional deacons preparing for ordination to the priesthood, except that their commitment to the work of a deacon endures throughout their life.

The diaconate is rooted in Christ the servant. Jesus had many titles and functions. He was teacher, Lord, priest, healer, and forgiver, to name a few. But deacons find their integration with Christ through his ministry as the one who came to be the servant of all. The Sacrament of Holy Orders confers an indelible spiritual character that cannot be repeated or conferred temporarily.[54] It imparts a sacramental grace for the fulfillment of a deacon's ministry.[55]

> The sacrament of Holy Orders marks [deacons] . . . with an *imprint* ("character") which cannot be removed and which configures them to Christ, who made himself the "deacon" or servant of all (CF. *Mk* 10:45; *Lk* 22:27; St. Polycarp, *Ad Phil.* 5, 2: SCh 10, 182).[56]

The sacramental grace that deacons receive "has a permanent virtuality. It flowers again and again in the same measure in which it is received and accepted again and again in faith."[57]

Consequently, the deacon must be a man of exceptional character. This was expected of him from the apostolic age, and it continues to this day. He takes on this office on the recommendation of the people of God, who give testimony to his worthiness during the Rite of Ordination.[58] At the ceremony he expresses his resolve to be consecrated a deacon and to discharge his duties "with humble charity in order to assist the priestly Order and to benefit the Christian people." He is "to hold fast to the mystery of faith with a clear conscience, as the Apostle urges, and to proclaim this faith in word and deed according to the Gospel and the Church's tradition."[59]

As a servant, Jesus obeyed his Father. Deacons first imitate that service during the Rite of Ordination when they kneel and place their joined hands in the hands of the Bishop. "In making his promise of respect and obedience to his Bishop, the deacon takes as his model Christ, who became the servant of his Father."[60]

The Bishop has a special relationship with the deacon. The deacon is ordained for service to him or to the superior of his religious community.[61] To show this relationship, only the Bishop imposes hands on the deacon in the Rite of Ordination.[62]

The deacon will help the Bishop exercise his responsibility to the entire community. The faithful are invited to the ordination ceremony to manifest the Church whom the deacon will serve, and to pray for the deacon especially during the Prayer of the Faithful.[63] The Bishop relies on their testimony to choose the deacon for service and to appoint him in the name of Christ to receive the gift of the Holy Spirit.[64]

Deacons may baptize.

The deacon will serve these people. His ordination incardinates him to the diocese: he makes a life-long commitment to serve this particular flock. With ordination he enters the clerical state, enhancing the service he devotes to the Church.[65]

The deacon exercises his ministry in three ways. He will assist at the liturgy, preach the Gospel, and perform charity. These duties are explained in the suggested homily from the *Rite of Ordination*.

As ministers of the altar, they will proclaim the Gospel, prepare the sacrifice, and distribute the Lord's Body and Blood to the faithful. Furthermore, it will be their duty, at the Bishop's direction, to exhort believers and unbelievers alike and to instruct them in holy doctrine. They will preside over public prayer, administer Baptism, assist at and bless Marriages, bring Viaticum to the dying, and conduct funeral rites. . . . [T]hey will perform works of charity in the name of the Bishop or the pastor. With the help of God, they are to go about all these duties in such a way that you will recognize them as disciples of him who came not to be served, but to serve.[66]

Other elements of the *Rite of Ordination* make the same point: when the deacon first puts on his liturgical vestments, when he receives the *Book of the Gospels,* and when he shares the kiss of peace.

By this investiture the liturgical ministry [that the deacons] will henceforth fulfill is outwardly manifested. The Handing on of the Book of Gospels signifies the office of the deacon to proclaim the Gospel in liturgical celebrations and to preach the faith of the Church in word and in deed. By the fraternal kiss the Bishop seals, so to speak, the deacons' admittance into his ministry. By the fraternal kiss the deacons present welcome the newly Ordained to a common ministry in their Order.[67]

At first glance, the prayer of ordination seems to focus on the liturgical ministry of the deacon,[68] as so many such prayers have done in the past. However, the prayer refers to two scriptural antecedents to the diaconate: the order of Levites in the Old Testament, and the selection of deacons to assist the apostles in the New Testament. The first of these was created for liturgical purposes, and the second for works of charity. Thus, the ordination prayer calls the deacons to fulfill their complete ministry.[69]

The final blessing of the Rite of Ordination (found in *The Roman Missal*) strengthens the deacons in each of these three functions.

> May God who has called you to the service of others
>   in his Church
> give you great zeal for all,
> especially the afflicted and the poor.
> Amen.

> May he, who has entrusted you with preaching the Gospel
>   of Christ,
> help you, as you live according to his word,
> to be its sincere and fervent witnesses.
> Amen.

> May he, who has appointed you stewards of his mysteries,
> make you imitators of his Son, Jesus Christ,
> and ministers of unity and peace in the world.
> Amen.

Many people associate the work of deacons with the liturgy. They may baptize, distribute Holy Communion, bring viaticum to the dying, expose the Blessed Sacrament and preside for Benediction, witness marriages, preside at funerals and burials, lead prayer service, and give blessings. But they may also deliver homilies, and it is expected that they will teach what they believe. They will also perform works of charity. Often these are done outside the public eye, but they are central to a deacon's ministry. Service to the community enhances preaching and liturgical leadership.

Questions for Discussion and Reflection

1. How did you first become interested in becoming a deacon?

_____

_____

2. Who inspired you in this ministry?

_____

_____

3. Why is the deacon's role important? How do you see the complete role of the deacon integrating into the Church's ministry?

_____

_____

NOTES

1. See Matthew 8:14–15.

2. See Matthew 27:55; Luke 8:3.

3. See Luke 10:40.

4. See Matthew 20:28; Mark 10:45.

5. See Luke 22:27.

6. See Mark 9:35.

7. See John 13:1–20.

8. See 1 Corinthians 12:4–5.

9. See Ephesians 4:11–12; 1 Peter 4:10–11 also encourages members of the community to serve with their gifts.

10. See 1 Corinthians 3:5; 2 Corinthians 3:6; 11:7–8, 23; Colossians 1:25.

11. See Romans 15:25.

12. See 1 Corinthians 16:15.

13. See Romans 16:1.

14. See Colossians 1:7; 4:7; Ephesians 6:21.

15. See 1 and 2 Timothy and Titus.

16. See 1 Timothy 3:8–13.

17. See 2 Timothy 4:5.

18. See Acts 12:25.

19. See Acts 8:4–14, 26–40.

20. See Acts 21:8.

21. See Acts 6:5.

22. See Acts 6:8–10.

23. See Acts 7:1–60.

24. See *Epistle of Clement of Rome to the Corinthians*, 42:4.

25. Ibid., 40:5.

26. See *Epistle of Ignatius of Antioch to the Magnesians*, 6:1, and to the Trallians 3:1.

27. See *Epistle of Ignatius to the Philadelphians*, 4:1.

28. See *Epistle of Ignatius to the Trallians*, 2:3.

29. See *Epistle of Polycarp to the Philippians*, 5:2–3.

30. Cyprian, Epistle 64.

31. Ibid., 32:1.

32. See *Apostolic Tradition*, 8:12.

33. Ibid., 39.

34. Ibid., 34.

35. Ibid., 21:12.

36. Ibid., 4.

37. See Eusebius, *History of the Church*, 6:43.

38. Epistle 146.

39. See Frederick Homes Dudden, *Gregory the Great, His Place in History and Thought* (New York and Bombay: Longmans, Green, and Co., 1905), vol. I, pp. 261–262.

40. See Isidore of Seville, *Letter to Leudefredus* (*Patrologia Latina*, 82:895).

41. See Michel Andrieu, *Les Ordines Romani* (hereafter, OR) 3:555–556, citing Gelasius' Epistles 14 and 15.

42. OR, 4:38, *Ordo* 35:26–28.

43. See *Sacramentarium Veronese* 950–951. The *Verona Sacramentary* is the oldest Catholic Roman ritual book in existence.

44. See, for example, Numbers 3:5–6.

45. See the *Gelasian Sacramentary* is the second oldest liturgical book in existence. It is usually dated from the eighth century.

46. See *Sacramentarium Gelasianum*, 156.

47. *Pontificale Romano-Germanicum*, 16:15.

48. Ibid., 16.17.

49. Pope Paul VI, *Ad pascendum;* translated by Paul Turner.

50. See Pope Pius XII, Apostolic Constitution, *Sacramentum ordinis*, November 30, 1947.

51. *Lumen gentium*, 29.

52. *Ad gentes*, 16.

53. June 18, 1967.

54. See *Catechism of the Catholic Church*, 1581.

55. See *Rite of Ordination of Deacons*, 173.

56. *Catechism of the Catholic Church*, 1570.

57. Congregation for Catholic Education; Congregation for Clergy, *Basic Norms for the Formation of Permanent Deacons* (1998), 7.

58. *Rite of Ordination*, 198.

59. Ibid., 200.

60. USCCB, *National Directory for the Formation, Ministry and Life of Permanent Deacons in the United States* (2005), 41.

61. See *Rite of Ordination*, 201.

62. Ibid., 206.

63. Ibid., 179.

64. Ibid., 1.

65. Ibid., 176.

66. Ibid., 199.

67. Ibid., 188.

68. Ibid., 207.

69. See the Congregation for Catholic Education, *Basic Norms for the Formation of Permanent Deacons*, 6.

The Spirituality of the Deacon

Sing to the LORD a new song;
sing to the LORD, all you lands.
Sing to the LORD; bless his name.
announce his salvation, day after day.
Tell his glory among the nations;
among all peoples, his wondrous deeds.

—*Psalm 96:1–3, Lectionary for Mass*

A deacon's spiritual life is rooted in the liturgy, the word of God, and in works of charity. A good deacon will develop all three aspects of his ministry, and seek ways to meet Christ more deeply in them all.

Saints

One way to develop the spiritual life is to reflect on the lives of some of the great deacons of the past. The Catholic Church's martyrology, or list of saints, includes quite a number of deacons. Meditation on their exemplary lives will help any deacon grow in Christ. Here are four of them.

Saint Stephen

At the top of the list stands Stephen. He heads the seven men chosen to be deacons in Acts 6. They were appointed at the request of the apostles to wait on tables. But their ministry grew. Stephen evangelized. He was filled with the Holy Spirit and worked miracles. His popularity created enemies among some of the religious leaders of his day. They accused him of blasphemy and had him arrested. According to Acts 7, Stephen gave an eloquent defense, showing how Jesus had fulfilled the promises of the old law. He also accused his accusers of not keeping the law. Meanwhile, he had a vision of the ascended Jesus at the right hand of God. The reaction against him was strong and fierce. His enemies dragged Stephen outside the city walls and stoned him to death. Just as Jesus had been falsely accused yet forgave his persecutors, so Stephen did the same. The murderers left their cloaks at the feet of a young man named Saul, who would continue the persecution until his own conversion, when he changed his name to Paul. Stephen's devoted followers buried his body.

Rocks purported to be those thrown at Stephen are on display as devotional articles in the Church of St. Lawrence outside the Walls of Rome.

How did I respond when I felt called to serve as a deacon? Do I disdain the little tasks that I am called to perform? Has my faith ever put me at risk? How? What dangers have I encountered because I chose to proclaim the Gospel? When have I taken the opportunity to speak about my faith? What was the reaction of those who heard me? What is my vision of Christ? When do I feel closest to him?

Saint Philip

Among the seven deacons in Acts 6 is Philip. He became known as an evangelizer and baptizer. He had success even in Samaria, a land known for its hostilities to Jews like Jesus. Philip converted Simon Magus, who accompanied him for a time, but then wrongly attempted to purchase the power of the Holy Spirit from the apostles. Simon's attempted misuse of funds for religious gains gave us the word simony.[1]

Later, while taking the desert road south of Jerusalem to Gaza, Philip boarded a chariot in which an Ethiopian official was riding. The man was reading from Isaiah, and Philip asked if he understood the passage. He admitted he needed a teacher. Philip seized the opportunity to explain how Isaiah foretold the coming of Jesus Christ and his saving death. As the conversation continued, the Ethiopian became a believer in Jesus. Spotting a pool of water from the chariot, he requested Baptism. Philip performed the ceremony, and then he vanished. The Ethiopian went on his way filled with the joy of faith.[2]

What has been my experience of preaching and baptizing? How have I felt as a minister of Baptism? Which aspects of this ministry are most appealing? Has my preaching ever failed to bring the conversion it intended? Have I seen people respond eagerly at first, but then withdraw from commitment? How has this made me feel? Where do I find my strength to go on? What is the field of my ministry? Like Philip, have I discovered that I am called to some people I never expected to serve? How would I describe my reaction? How have I seen the hand of Christ in my ministry?

Saint Lawrence

One of the most important saints of the early Church was Lawrence. In the city of Rome more churches are named for him than for any other saint except Mary. He served in Rome as one of the seven deacons who helped administer churches and provided for the poor. He was martyred during the persecution of Valerian in the middle of the third century. Few historical details are certain, but legends have endured.

Before suffering martyrdom, Pope Sixtus II told his deacon that he would follow in just a few days. Sobered by these words, in a final act of charity, Lawrence sold all the precious vessels of the church and gave the money to the city's poor. Valerian's army, unawares, asked him to turn over the Church's precious vessels for the needs of the State. Lawrence agreed, and established a meeting date and time. Meanwhile, he gathered up the poor of the city. Then he presented to his persecutors the real treasures of the Church—the poor.

Predictably, Valerian was outraged. He prepared a painful martyrdom for Lawrence. Coals were lit beneath an iron grill. Lawrence was stripped and placed on top to roast. He experienced no pain, and his body emitted light and a pleasing aroma. After a while, he told his persecutors, "Turn me over. I'm done on this side."

What responsibilities am I accepting in the office of deacon? Do my ordinary tasks have a deeper spiritual meaning? How do I minister to the poor? What is my attitude to the poor? In what way are they the treasures of the Church? In what way are they the treasures of my life? What would I be willing to die for? For my wife? My children? My parents? My friends? Would I be willing to lay down my life for my faith? Would I do it for the poor? What has been the most difficult task I have been asked to do in my service to the Church? Why was it so hard?

Saint Francis of Assisi

Born into a wealthy family, Francis learned the cloth trade of his father and enjoyed a profligate youth in the early thirteenth century. While

praying at Saint Damian in Assisi, he heard Jesus speak to him from the church's cross. The voice asked him to rebuild the church. Francis began making repairs on three churches in Assisi until he realized he was being called to rebuild the interior life of Christians. He gave away all his possessions, renounced his inheritance, helped the poor, and lived simply. Surprisingly, he attracted a large number of followers. Eventually he sought and received approval from Pope Innocent III for their rule of life.

Francis was ordained a deacon. His ordination recognized his authority within the community, while it honored his desire not to become a priest. Francis greatly respected priests, but he felt unworthy to join their ranks.

Francis was so committed to renunciation and repentance that he carried the message on missionary journeys. He greatly desired to convert Muslims. Late in his life Francis received the stigmata, the wounds of the crucified Jesus, upon his own body. His love of nature is retold in stories of how he preached to birds and tamed a wolf; it is best recognized in his poem, the "Canticle of the Sun," which he completed shortly before his death.

If I am to live faithfully as a deacon, what must I renounce? Which of my possessions and habits is keeping me from following the Gospel of Christ? To whom am I called to bring this Gospel? Who most needs to hear the message that has taken root in my heart? What actions will I take to bring the Gospel there? What will my message be? How do I show respect for the earth? How will my diaconate be a symbol that honors the creator of all things? How do I look upon my forthcoming death? How will it be an expression of the service I am called to give as a deacon?

Proclaiming the Gospel

One of the most memorable lines of the *Rite of Ordination* for deacons is the one concerning the Gospel. As the Bishop places the *Book of the Gospels* in the hands of the deacon, he says, "Receive the Gospel of Christ, whose herald you have become. Believe what you read, teach what you believe, and practice what you teach."[3]

How did I first come to believe the Gospel? Who proclaimed it to me? Which stories about Christ have struck me during my life? Why have they seemed so important? In what ways am I a herald of the Gospel? How have I proclaimed the Gospel with my words? With my deeds? When in my life have I found myself proclaiming the Good News?

Take some time to reacquaint yourself with the Gospel. One way to do this is to set aside an hour or so for some personal prayer. Take a Bible with you, go to your church, and sit in the presence of the Blessed Sacrament. Read all of Mark's account of the Gospel. It's the shortest, and most likely the oldest, of the four. Dwell especially on the very first line, where Mark explains that he is going to relate the Gospel. It's probably the first time the word was used for a literary composition. Mark coins the word "Gospel." As you read the entire book, come back in your mind to his first statement. Ask yourself along the way, "How is this Good News?" "Who is Jesus Christ the Son of God for me?" "How do I proclaim this Gospel?"

"Receive the Gospel of Christ, whose herald you have become."

Deacons and Angels

In the history of western art, angels are often depicted wearing dalmatics, the liturgical vesture of deacons. The practice came from a spiritual mixing of the responsibilities of each group.

Two of the Gospel accounts conclude the story of the temptation of Jesus by saying that angels came and ministered to him.[4] In both cases, the Greek verb is *diekonoun*. You could say the angels "deaconed" Jesus. The service that deacons give could be described as a helping ministry to Christ, a mission that angels performed from the very start of his public ministry.

Shortly after his triumphal entry into Jerusalem, Jesus spoke about his coming death and the glory of God's name. He heard the voice of his Father, which some thought was thunder, but others believed was the voice of an angel.[5] When Jesus was arrested, he stated that the Father could send legions of angels to rescue him.[6] But that was not his mission. These incidents indicate that angels existed to serve the needs of Jesus.

Deacons have taken the role of ministers of the cup.

Poignantly, an angel did appear to Jesus at Gethsemane. He asked the Father to remove the cup, if it was the Father's will. An angel appeared to strengthen him. Jesus prayed again, and his sweat fell to the ground like great drops of blood.[7] This passage does not appear in all bibles, but the overlaying themes of cup, blood, and angel have all contributed to the idea that deacons share in the ministry of angels. Some artists depict angels holding cups that collect the blood flowing from the side of Christ as he hangs upon the cross. In the liturgy, deacons have taken the role of ministers of the cup.

The word "angel" literally means "messenger." In Greek it is *aggelos* (the first "g" is pronounced like an "n"), and it is related to the word *euaggelios,* which means "good news" and is commonly translated as "Gospel." According to Luke, for example, Gabriel tells Mary that she has been chosen to be the mother of God's Son.[8] Angels proclaim Good News, and in their ministry, deacons proclaim the Gospel.

One reason artists began depicting angels in dalmatics was to show their relationship to the ministry of deacons. Just as deacons assist priests at the altar, so angels assist God. For example, Raphael appears in the book of Tobit to help Tobias run errands that lead to the recovery of his father's sight and the meeting of his own future bride. Angels perform the menial tasks of those who do not scale the ladders of success. In some Eastern rite liturgies, deacons assist at the altar with ceremonial fans. They wave them gently through the air in imitation of great wings.

Just as angels accompanied Jesus in his Passion, so did one appear to announce his Resurrection. According to Matthew, an angel rolled away the stone in front of the tomb, sat upon it, radiated light, struck fear in the guards, and calmed the visiting women with the first proclamation of the ultimate Good News: "Jesus is not here. He has risen." They also commissioned the women to tell the Good News to the other disciples.[9]

Angels performed similar functions in other passages of the Bible. In the Old Testament, an angel brings Elijah food and drink on his flight from the murderous Jezebel in Samaria to the protective God on Mount Horeb.[10] In the book of Daniel, Nebuchadnezzar threw into the fiery furnace three young men who refused to deny their faith. He was astonished to see them all alive, and a fourth figure, an angel of God, protecting them from death.[11] In the New Testament, when Stephen the deacon was arrested, his face appeared like that of an angel.[12]

Because angels rescued so many faithful people from their suffering, and explicitly assisted Jesus in his Passion and Resurrection, deacons minister at the altar for the celebration of the Mass. They assist at the sacrifice, just as angels do.

In my life, when have I suffered most greatly? How did God send me a strengthening angel? How does my ministry relieve the suffering of others? How have I proclaimed Good News to those who needed the message the most? If my ministry to the Church is like that of the angels, how should I live? How should I act? How should I intervene? How will I hear what God commands you to do? How am I God's messenger?

The Chalice

In the Rite of Ordination, the new deacons are invited to assist at the Liturgy of the Eucharist, "particularly by offering the chalice."[13] The chalice is one of the main responsibilities of the deacon.

At a typical Mass, the deacon prepares the chalice by pouring wine and a little water into it.[14] At the end of the Eucharistic Prayer, he elevates the chalice while the priest elevates the vessel of consecrated bread.[15] At Communion time, the deacon receives under both forms.[16] He then offers the chalice of the precious blood to the faithful.[17] The deacon purifies the chalice and other vessels after Communion.[18]

The association of the deacon with the ministry of the chalice may have originated as a practical matter. It takes two ministers to offer the Body and Blood of Christ to the faithful. The priest and deacon probably shared these responsibilities from the start. However, the practice of offering the cup may relate to the deacon's providing for the needs of the poor and the hungry. As the first deacons served meals to the community, so today's deacons serve the spiritual hunger and thirst of the faithful.

The ministry of the cup may have been enhanced by an allegorical interpretation of the strengthening angel who assisted Jesus at the time of his Passion. This angel appeared precisely when Jesus asked for the cup to pass from him. As his sweat fell like drops of blood, the strengthening angel helped Jesus to drink the cup of the Father's divine plan. Deacons perform a similar function for the faithful.

How do I fulfill the physical and spiritual thirst of the people around you? What are they thirsty for? What do I have that brings them refreshment? How do I offer it to them? Who in my ministry has a difficult cup to drink? Is it a cup of sorrow, of pain, of fear, or remorse? How am I, as a minister of the chalice, called to bring them relief?

Directions and Announcements

The deacon also gives directions to the people regarding the offering of peace[19] and the time for dismissal.[20] He may state the intentions of the Prayer of the Faithful.[21] He may make the announcements that conclude the service.[22]

These responsibilities help clarify the roles of both the priest and the deacon. When the deacon is giving directions to the faithful during the liturgy, he frees the priest from the business of the orderly execution of the Mass. The deacon manages the actions of other ministers and the congregation. This allows the priest to concentrate more intently on his own role. The priest is to lead the people at prayer during the liturgy. If he also gives directions to others, it can draw his focus away from his primary work. With a deacon at his side, the priest more naturally gives only this instruction to the people: "Let us pray." Meanwhile, the deacon lessens the distractions and makes prayer more possible.

It is important for the priest and the deacon to work together at the liturgy. By their collaboration, they help everyone to exercise the ministry for which each is responsible.

By leading the Prayer of the Faithful and making the announcements, the deacon clarifies his own role inside and outside the liturgy. To do either of these effectively, the deacon needs to know what is happening in the parish and in the world, and to bring these issues into dialogue with worship.

After the priest introduces the Prayer of the Faithful, the deacon lists the petitions. The people respond to each. The priest concludes the petitions with a prayer. The deacon tells the people what they should pray for. To do this with integrity, he needs to know the needs. He should be actively engaged in service outside the liturgy. He informs the people from his own experience what most requires their prayer.

When the deacon makes announcements, he tells the people about opportunities for service that await them in the coming week. He will do this with integrity if he himself is familiar with these events and should be well acquainted with parish organizations and services. When he informs the community about them, his voice commands attention. He will gain a response if he himself is immersed in service to the Church outside the liturgy. In a sense, the first person for whom the announcements exist is the deacon. They remind him of his responsibilities, and he invites others to share his diaconal ministry. He brings these announcements to a fitting close when he dismisses the assembly. He does not merely announce that Mass is over; he proclaims that service has begun.

When I participate at Mass, how do I unite service and worship? What aspects of my service particularly suit my ministry at the altar? How do I learn about the needs of the community? How might I do this better? How do I learn about the service opportunities of the community? How might I do this better?

Liturgy of the Hours

During the Rite of Ordination, the deacon affirms his desire to pray the Liturgy of the Hours.[23] He does this not just for himself, but for the entire people of God. And not just for the entire people of God, but for the entire human race.[24]

The Liturgy of the Hours consecrates the times of the day. It relies heavily on the book of Psalms as a vehicle for prayer. It highlights readings from the Bible, and it raises prayers for the needs of the community, the Church and the world.

To pray the Liturgy of the Hours is to join the voice of the universal Church, consecrating the hours of the day to God. Especially at sunrise and sunset, as the world alternates between darkness and light, when the edges of life are ill-defined, it is time to pray.

What is my habit of daily prayer? How do I pray? What materials do I use? With whom do I pray? How do I mark the turnings of day and night? How do I sanctify the arrival of a new week? How do I honor the liturgical times?

Celibacy, Marriage, and Widowhood

For some men, ordination to the diaconate includes a commitment to celibacy. Pope Paul VI affirmed the value of celibacy in his reflection on its purpose in the life of the priest. The main points apply to deacons as well.

Jesus himself was celibate, and he consecrated his entire life to the will of the Father, placing himself at the service of others. Jesus lived for the sake of the kingdom, and he promised a special recompense for those who forsook wife and children for that same purpose. He invited followers into a new way of life. Celibacy stimulates a charity that is open to all. It increases a person's ability to listen to the word of God and to pray. A celibate's sacrificial love inspires others to faithful chastity. Celibacy gives ministry freedom and flexibility. It points a pilgrim people toward the kingdom where people will live in total freedom and love of God.[25]

Many deacons minister as married men. In doing so, they bring their commitment to their wives into their service of the Church. Their experience of marriage enhances their work for the Church, and their service as a deacon enhances their commitment to marriage. A married deacon shows the love of Christ both personally and professionally. He calls others to a more joyful and dedicated commitment to married love.

> Married deacons should feel especially obliged to give clear witness to the sanctity of marriage and the family. The more they grow in mutual love, the greater their dedication to their children and the more significant their example for the Christian community.[26]

A deacon who suffers the death of a wife enters a world of sorrow and hope. The loss of a life partner who has strengthened his faith will doubtless bring profound grief to a man who has loved and served well. At the same time, faith in the Resurrection will comfort the deacon on the occasion of his loss. He becomes all the more a sign of faith and hope for those in the world who face the mysteries of love and death.

God has called me to a particular state of life, whether it be single or married. How have I responded to this call? How does it enhance my life? How does it express my faith? How am I a symbol of hope to others?

NOTES

1. See Acts 8:4–25.

2. See Acts 8:26–39.

3. *Rite of Ordination*, 210.

4. See Matthew 4:11; Mark 1:13.

5. See John 12:27–29.

6. See Matthew 26:53.

7. See Luke 22:42–44.

8. See Luke 1:35.

9. See Matthew 28:1–8.

10. See 1 Kings 19:5-8.

11. See Daniel 3:28.

12. See Acts 6:15.

13. *Rite of Ordination*, 189.

14. See The Order of Mass from the third edition of *The Roman Missal*, 24; *General Instruction of the Roman Missal* (GIRM), 178.

15. See GIRM, 180.

16. See GIRM, 182.

17. Ibid.

18. See GIRM, 183.

19. See GIRM, 181.

20. See GIRM, 185.

21. See GIRM, 71.

22. See GIRM, 184.

23. *Rite of Ordination*, 178.

24. Ibid.

25. See Pope Paul VI, Encyclical on the Celibacy of the Priest, 17–34.

26. Congregation for the Clergy, *Directory for the Ministry and Life of Priests*, 61.

Serving as the Deacon

The Deacon at the Celebration of Mass

The Eucharist "contains the entire spiritual boon of the Church, that is, Christ himself, our Pasch and Living Bread . . . ."[1] These words of the Second Vatican Council are affirmed in the *General Instruction of the Roman Missal* (GIRM), which notes that at the celebration of the Mass (as the action of Christ and the People of God arrayed hierarchically), we find the center of Christian life for the universal and local Church, as well as for each of us individually.[2] Clearly, the Mass is the "center and high point" of our faith,[3] the action by which God sanctifies the world in Christ, and the primary way we worship, praise, and give thanks to the Father, adoring him through Christ, the Son of God, in the Holy Spirit. All sacred actions and all activities of Christian life are bound up with the Eucharist, flow from the Eucharist and are ordered to the Eucharist.[4]

So, too, does the Eucharist constitute the fundamental core of a deacon's identity and ministry. His three-fold ministry to the Word, liturgy, and charity flow from the grace and gift of the Mass. It is the Eucharist from which the deacon's ministry flows.

Deacons are charged with specific duties and responsibilities at Mass—ministerial functions proper to their office—and different from the presidential functions of the Priest Celebrant, including actions, postures, and gestures. Whenever a deacon is present at any celebration of Mass, he should exercise his office. It is important to offer this for reflection to other liturgical ministers who participate in the Mass as an opportunity to understand the deacon's role in the liturgy. If ministry is done in collaboration, with a theological understanding of the roles of various ministers at Mass, then it can never appear to some that a deacon is taking away duties from a lay minister at the altar when he is, in fact, simply exercising his office as prescribed by the liturgical books.

Prior to Mass with a Deacon

A deacon's altar ministry begins long before the Entrance Procession. As the priest's assistant, the deacon should ensure that all the necessary sacred vessels, liturgical books, and other materials are in their proper places prior to Mass. This preparation may be done collaboratively with sacristans, altar servers, lectors and readers, and other liturgical ministers. But as the Priest Celebrant's primary assistant at Mass, the deacon should always ensure that everything is readied for the celebration about to take place. For example, deacons should mark the passage proper to the day's liturgical celebration in the *Book of the Gospels*, if used; mark the appropriate pages in *The Roman Missal* (this includes the Collect, Prayer over the Offerings, Prayer after Communion, and the proper Preface for the Eucharistic Prayer); place the *Lectionary for Mass* on the ambo and mark the proper readings; be familiar with the Lectionary in case the lector or reader loses the bookmark and needs assistance while at the ambo; check that the sacred vessels are in place on the credence table (celebrant's chalice, Holy Communion cups, paten, and ciboria, if needed); ensure that other articles are provided as needed: corporal, chalice veil and pall, cruet of water, purificators, and lavabo with towel for the washing of hands; prepare the assembly's gift table with a ciborium (ciboria) filled with communion hosts and a flagon (or cruet) with wine; check that altar candles are lit, and that the deacon's chair is to the right of the celebrant's chair; and make sure the hymnals or worship aids for both deacon and the priest are available.

Deacons always should vest properly for assisting at Mass. Deacons wear "the alb, the stole and the dalmatic; the latter may be omitted, however, either out of necessity or on account of a lesser degree of solemnity. . . . All who wear an alb should use a cincture and an amice, unless, due to the form of the alb, they are not needed."[5] *Redemptionis sacramentum* also states that "The proper vestment of the Deacon is the dalmatic, to be worn over an alb and stole. In order that the beautiful tradition of the Church may be preserved, it is praiseworthy to refrain from exercising the option of omitting the dalmatic."[6] Refer to the *Ordo* for the proper vestment color.[7]

Now everything is ready for Mass, the altar servers and other liturgical ministers are in place, and the deacon is ready to assist the priest at the start of the Sunday liturgy.

Introductory Rites

These rites begin the public prayer of the Church, and have the character of beginning, introduction, and preparation. The purpose is to help the assembly come together as one in the presence of God and dispose themselves to listen properly to God's word and to celebrate the Eucharist worthily.

The beginning of the Mass demands its own attention, reverence, and dignity. As the mystery of Christ's sacrifice is to be re-presented to all believers for the first time and yet again, deacons should model for the assembly the awe and wonder that is a part of this gift and grace. This reminds us that the celebration of the Eucharist is the preeminent expression of the Church itself.

The deacon carries the *Book of the Gospels* slightly elevated and precedes the priest (but behind other liturgical ministers) in the procession to the altar. Without the *Book of the Gospels*, the deacon is to walk at the priest's side (customarily on the right). It might be important to review a few additional protocols here. If there are concelebrants present and one deacon with the *Book of the Gospels*, he processes in front of the concelebrants. If there are two deacons, the deacon of the Word carries the *Book of the Gospels*, walking in front of the celebrant/concelebrants; the deacon of the Eucharist walks at the celebrant's right side. If there are two deacons and no *Book of the Gospels*, deacons walk on either side of the celebrant. Finally, if a *Book of the Gospels* is not used, no other liturgical book should be carried in the procession, either by a deacon or lay person. This means the Lectionary should at all times remain on the ambo and never be part of the Entrance Procession.

Upon reaching the sanctuary, and if carrying the *Book of the Gospels*, the deacon omits the sign of reverence (no genuflection or profound bow), and goes up to the altar immediately—not waiting for the rest of the ministers—places the *Book of the Gospels* flat on its surface in an appropriate place (center of the altar), steps back, and waits until the Priest Celebrant reaches the altar so that they together may venerate it with a kiss. Without the *Book of the Gospels*, he makes a profound bow to the altar with the priest in the customary way (if the tabernacle is in the sanctuary, both priest and deacon genuflect instead), and then, with the priest, venerates the altar with a kiss. (Remember that the altar is both a table of sacrifice and the table of the Paschal banquet; it is a symbol of Christ himself. Veneration recalls that it is holy and sacred to the action of the assembly.)

If incense is used, the deacon assists the priest by putting some incense into the thurible (by holding the boat), and walks slightly behind and to the priest's right as the priest incenses the cross and altar. If the Priest Celebrant does not want assistance, the deacon should stand attentively behind the altar, ready to accept the thurible from him after incensation.

The deacon hands the thurible to a server, then moves to his chair and stands next to the priest, taking his place "at the priest's side and assists him as necessary."[8] This means whether there is a single Priest Celebrant, concelebrants, or even a Bishop celebrant, the deacon sits next to the celebrant, customarily on his right.

The Sign of the Cross is perhaps the oldest gesture of our faith. It is the traditional prelude to prayer, and a self-blessing with strong baptismal overtones. The deacon makes the Sign of the Cross with the celebrant and assembly.

As the Priest Celebrant extends his hands and offers the greeting ("The grace of our Lord Jesus Christ . . . ," etc.) to the people, the deacon stands with hands folded. A quick look at *The Roman Missal* indicates that this extended-hands gesture is a presidential function, not a ministerial one. Deacons do not extend their hands or make gestures in any manner during the greeting.

After the greeting, the deacon may introduce the Mass to the people. This should be a very brief introduction, not an opportunity for a mini-homily or announcements.

The priest invites the assembly to participate in the Penitential Act, which they do either through a recitation of an act of contrition or through a formula of invocations.

The deacon may offer the invocations in Option III of the Penitential Act. Also, he may write his own tropes; but the deacon must remember that these are invocations directed to Christ, thanking and praising him for what he has done for his people. They are not exclamations that tell the Lord something about us and our need. Also note the Penitential Act gives the faithful time to recall sins in preparation for the unity of the Eucharist. Therefore, deacons should pause for a moment before starting the invocations. Everyone should understand that the forgiveness rendered here "lacks the efficacy of the Sacrament of Penance."[9]

Unless Option III is used, the Kyrie follows the Penitential Act.

If the Rite of Blessing and Sprinkling of Water is used in place of the Penitential Act, the deacons may assist the celebrant with *The Roman Missal* and carry the situla (or water container) when the priest sprinkles the people. When completed, the Kyrie is omitted.

The Gloria is a joyful song, a hymn of praise glorifying God, found in Christian prayer books as early as the fourth century! It was originally sung only on feast days; now it is offered on Sundays outside of Advent and Lent (except if All Souls' Day falls on a Sunday), on solemnities and feasts, and in solemn local celebrations. It originates from the Christmas narrative in the Gospel according to Luke. The deacon sings or recites the hymn with the assembly.

The priest then offers the Collect—he"collects" the prayers of the faithful and offers them to God. The deacon may hold *The Roman Missal* for the celebrant.

Liturgy of the Word

The deacon sits at his chair (feet flat on floor, palms on thighs, or hands on his knees) and listens to the First Reading, where God speaks to his chosen people. An Old Testament proclamation manifests that all scripture is the word of God, and points to the coming of Jesus. Deacons only proclaim this reading if no other reader is present.

The deacon joins in singing or praying the Responsorial Psalm with the assembly. Here the Christian community uses God's word to respond to God's word—the Psalm "fosters meditation on the Word of God."[10]

The deacon will move before the celebrant, profoundly bow, and ask for a blessing.

The deacon continues to sit and listen to the Second Reading. Note that the New Testament reading helps the assembly encounter the early Church living the Christian faith. The witness of the apostolic community is an example for us all, and for all times. Again, the deacon proclaims this reading only if no other lector or reader is present.

If incense is used during the Alleluia or other Gospel Acclamation, the deacon assists the Priest Celebrant by holding the boat. Then with hands folded, he moves before the celebrant, profoundly bows, and says, "Your blessing, Father." The priest speaks words and blesses him with the Sign of the Cross, at which time the deacon crosses himself, and responds, "Amen." He approaches the altar, profoundly bows, picks up the *Book of the Gospels*, and processes to the ambo carrying the book slightly elevated; he is preceded by the thurifer and candle bearers. (In some parishes, this Gospel procession is quite elaborate. If you are not familiar with the parish's custom, inquire before Mass begins.)

Placing the book on the ambo, the deacon, with hands joined, offers the greeting, announces the reading, signs the book with his thumb, signs himself (forehead, lips, and breast), incenses the book (three sets of two swings—center, left, then right), and proclaims the Gospel. The deacon should bow to the *Book of the Gospels* before and after he incenses it.

After the proclamation, the deacon kisses the book, saying quietly, "Through the words of the Gospel / may our sins be wiped away." If a Bishop is the celebrant, he may take the book for him to kiss or to impart a blessing. (Consult with a Bishop prior to Mass so that you know his preference.) Then the deacon returns the book to a place of honor, or places in on the credence table, and returns to sit in his chair.

Note that the deacon is the special minister to proclaim this sacred reading which recounts the words and deeds of Christ. That's because its reading is a ministerial function—not a presidential function. The tradition of the deacon's proclamation of the Gospel goes back to the ancient Church. Only in the absence of a deacon or concelebrants does the primary celebrant proclaim the Gospel.

A deacon may offer the homily; it should be given standing at the ambo. It is important to remember that the faculty to preach gives deacons a right to do so, but the pastor must give permission to do so. A Sunday homily is not to be omitted without serious reason; and it is reserved to ordained ministers. After the homily, the deacon returns and sits in the chair, silently reflecting with the assembly on the Gospel and its meaning and application to lived experiences.

All stand together to profess our faith through the Creed, a prayer that summarizes all that Catholic Christians believe. It is said on Sunday, solemnities, and solemn local celebrations. The deacon (and the entire assembly) profoundly bows at the words "And by the Holy Spirit was incarnate . . ." because the Incarnation is the most sacred moment of all creation. (However, "on the Solemnities of the Annunciation and the Nativity of the Lord, all genuflect."[11])

GIRM, 177 states: "After the introduction by the Priest, it is the Deacon himself who announces the intentions of the Universal Prayer, usually from the ambo." There is a theological explanation for this rubric. As part of his threefold ministry of service to word, liturgy, and charity, the deacon is to be that link between clergy and laity. In ministering to the people of the parish, he surfaces their needs, both spiritual and practical; then he brings these needs to the attention of the parish community, especially at liturgy. This also is why the deacon could be responsible for writing the Prayers of the Faithful for the parish. He can work with liturgical preparation or worship teams in doing so, but it should be understood that this is an essential part of his ministerial responsibility at Mass.

Liturgy of the Eucharist

This portion of the Mass includes two theological cores—the Eucharistic meal which Jesus gave to us as his memorial, and the Hebrew tradition of sacrifice offered to God. All eyes now focus on the altar, where the table is prepared, and gifts are set apart and presented as a sign that the community desires to incorporate itself in the sacrifice of Christ. Thus, the Mass is re-presenting (happening for the first time, again) of the Last Supper (Holy Thursday) and the sacrifice on the Cross (Good Friday).

The Liturgy of the Eucharist begins with the Presentation and the Preparation of the Gifts. While the priest remains at the chair, the deacon prepares the altar; he may be assisted by altar servers, but the deacon has responsibility alone to care for sacred vessels. Altar preparation includes placing upon the altar a corporal, *The Roman Missal*, chalice, and purificator; accompanying the celebrant as he receives the gifts from the people (a deacon may hand gifts to acolytes, if there are several ciboria offered; however, a deacon should not take gifts directly from the people); handing the paten with bread to the priest; pouring wine into the chalice(s) and/or Communion cups, and a little water only into the celebrant's chalice while saying inaudibly, "By the mystery of this water and wine / may we come to share in the divinity of Christ / who humbled himself to share in our humanity." Then he hands the chalice to the celebrant. (This commingling of water and wine is meant to signify the divine and human nature of Christ joined together in the Incarnation.) If incense is used, he holds the boat while assisting the priest with the thurible; he may accompany the celebrant as he incenses the altar and cross. Upon completion, he accepts the thurible from the priest, incenses the celebrant, concelebrants (if any), and the assembly with three swings of the censor (the same as when he incensed the *Book of the Gospels*). When incensing the assembly, the deacon bows to the people before and after the incensation. When finished, he hands the thurible to the acolyte and joins the priest standing at the altar. (During this action, acolytes assist the celebrant with the washing of the hands—a sign of purification in preparation for the most sacred part of the Mass.) During the Prayer over the Offerings, the deacon stands at the altar with hands folded.

The Eucharistic Prayer begins with the Preface. During the Preface, the celebrant makes gestures at the altar while speaking. Deacons keep their hands joined. The priest's gestures are a presidential function, and not part of the deacon's ministry.

During the body of the Eucharistic Prayer, a deacon stands near but slightly behind the celebrant (and customarily on the right) so that he may assist the priest. Some celebrants may ask you to turn the pages of *The Roman Missal*; then the deacon stands to his left.

Close proximity also is demanded during concelebrated Masses, when one or more (sometimes very many!) concelebrants gather around the altar during the Eucharistic Prayer. Rather than move far behind the concelebrants or get lost in the crowd, deacons should review GIRM, 215. This article reminds concelebrants that as they approach the altar and stand around it, they should not obstruct the execution of the rites nor obstruct the

✠ After the Prayer over the Offerings has been said by the principal celebrant, the concelebrants approach the altar and stand around it, but in such a way that they do not obstruct the execution of the rites and that the sacred action may be seen clearly by the faithful. Nor should they obstruct the Deacon whenever he needs to approach the altar by reason of his ministry.

The Deacon exercises his ministry near the altar, assisting whenever necessary with the chalice and the Missal. However, in so far as possible, he stands back slightly, behind the concelebrating Priests standing around the principal celebrant.

—*GIRM, 215*

sacred action to be seen by the faithful. A special admonition goes further: They should not be in the deacon's way whenever he needs to go to the altar.

Although the GIRM goes on to say that in so far as possible, the deacon stands back slightly, behind the concelebrating priests who stand around the principal celebrant, most concelebrants know that it is impossible for deacons to see through bodies. Therefore, it is good for concelebrants to leave a space for the deacon so that they are not blocking his sight of what is happening at the altar nor preventing him from moving easily up to the altar to receive the chalice from the celebrant to hold up during the doxology.

From the epiclesis (before the consecration) until the priest shows the chalice after the consecration, the deacon normally remains kneeling. This means the instruction to kneel is not imperative but normative. When might a deacon remain standing instead of kneeling during this portion of the Eucharistic Prayer? Only if he is physically incapable of kneeling, or if he will struggle greatly to kneel and stand; otherwise he may draw attention to himself and away from the sacramental action on the altar. Also worth noting, if more than one deacon is assisting at Mass, they should consult prior to the liturgy and decide if both can kneel or if they must stand. Regardless of the decision, which should be guided by the intent of the GIRM, both deacons should either kneel or stand, thereby not drawing attention to themselves.

GIRM, 179, notes that if several deacons are present, one of them may place incense in the thurible for the consecration and incense the host and chalice as they are shown to the people. This action takes place infrequently, and then usually during a Mass led by a Bishop. While not much used, deacons and other liturgical ministers should be aware of this option.

It is the presidential function of the celebrant to recite the Eucharistic Prayer. Deacons should never speak the prayer along with the celebrant, or move their lips so as to appear reciting the prayer with the priest. Deacons do not introduce the Memorial Acclamation ("The mystery of faith"). This is a presidential function that belongs to the priest alone. Deacons sing or recite the Memorial Acclamation with the faithful. During the final doxology, the deacon should elevate the chalice in silence after it has been given to him by the celebrant, and until he and the people respond, "Amen." Even with concelebrants, the deacon elevates the chalice during the doxology. It also is important for deacons to consider their gestures, as well as postures, during the Eucharistic Prayer. The celebrant, as part of his presidential function, says many words and makes many gestures specific to his particular ministry. These include movements with his hands, bowing, and genuflections. Such gestures are not part of the ministerial function of the deacon. Unless the deacon is unable to kneel during the Eucharistic Prayer, the deacon's only posture is to stand or kneel attentively while his only gesture is to do so with hands joined. However, if the deacon does not kneel, he should make a profound bow as the priest genuflects (see GIRM, 43). The deacon makes no gestures with his hands during the Eucharistic Prayer, makes no bows as the priest elevates the bread and wine during the consecration.

Communion Rite

The Communion Rite serves to help properly dispose those who will receive the Body and Blood of Christ. The deacon's role in this part of the liturgy is to assist the priest, and help the people do just that.

The deacon recites the Lord's Prayer with the assembly. The embolism ("Deliver us, Lord, we pray, from every evil . . .") elaborates on the last petition of the Lord's Prayer, and is spoken by the priest alone. The deacon joins the assembly in the doxology or response ("For the kingdom, the power, and the glory . . ."). Note that the proper gesture for deacons during the Lord's Prayer is hands joined. The orans position (arms extended) is a presidential gesture; this is not an option offered to the deacon in his ministerial role.

Now the Church asks for peace and unity for herself and the whole human family, and the assembly expresses to each other their ecclesial communion and mutual charity before receiving Eucharist. It has been part of the Mass since the fourth century. After the priest has said the prayer at the sign of peace and its greeting, and the people have responded, the deacon, if it is appropriate, invites all to exchange the sign of peace. He does this by facing the people, and with hands joined, saying, "Let us offer each other the sign of peace."

The phrase "if appropriate" refers to whether the sign of peace will be offered at all; it does not mean that someone other then the deacon should make this invitation.

As noted, the deacon should make the invitation facing the people. This means he must be near the altar so people can both see and hear his invitation. If there are many concelebrants, and the deacon is standing slightly behind the priests, he must make his way through the crowd to offer the invitation. The deacon should never intone the instructions from behind a row of concelebrants, or far behind the altar. Concelebrants should be instructed ahead of time to leave room for the deacon to come up to the altar to invite people to offer the sign of peace.

As he makes the invitation to the people, the deacon is to do so with hands joined. This is, again, an instruction that the deacon make no hand gestures during this invitation, no waving or grand sweep of the arms to seemingly include the entire assembly in this invitation. All are invited by the words alone.

GIRM, 181, notes that the deacon receives the sign of peace from the priest. Deacons should be aware of GIRM, 239, which states that if concelebrants are present, they receive the sign of peace from the priest before the deacon does: "After the Deacon or, in the absence of a Deacon, one of the concelebrants, has given the instruction *Let us offer each other the sign of peace*, all give one another the Sign of Peace. Those concelebrants nearer the principal celebrant receive the Sign of Peace from him before the Deacon does." Finally, GIRM, 181, states that after receiving the sign of peace from the priest, he may offer it to those other ministers who are close to him. This means that the deacon should not venture far from his spot in the sanctuary to engage in the sign of peace, nor should he (or the priest) leave the sanctuary to offer the sign of peace to members of the assembly, except in exceptional circumstance.

The fractioning of the bread recalls Christ's action at table with his apostles at the Last Supper, so the Priest Celebrant takes the host and breaks it over the paten. It also signifies that the many faithful are made one body by receiving Holy Communion from the one Bread of Life, which is Christ, who died and rose for the salvation of the world. GIRM, 83, gives permission to the deacon (or concelebrants) to assist in this rite, if needed. It also notes that the rite should be carried out with proper reverence, not be unnecessarily prolonged, nor given undue importance. If the deacon does assist the priest in the fraction, he should be familiar with the manner in which the consecrated bread is broken, and do so over a paten or ciborium, which should be laying on a corporal in case elements of the consecrated bread should fragment. Given the large number of vessels placed on the altar to accommodate the reception of Holy Communion under both species, many parishes have begun using extra large corporals to catch any particles of the host or drops of Precious Blood, which may occur when using these vessels.

The Lamb of God is sung or said, and may be repeated until the breaking of the bread is completed.

The deacon receives under both species after the priest has received. If concelebrants are present, the concelebrants consume the host with the Priest Celebrant. The Priest Celebrant then gives Holy Communion to the deacon.

Should deacons only minister the cup when the Eucharist is offered under both species? Not necessarily. GIRM, 182, relates that when Holy Communion is given under both species, the deacon administers the chalice to the communicants. However, the GIRM does not prohibit the deacon from offering the Body of Christ to the faithful. The general rule of thumb for deacons is to normally administer the chalice whenever the congregation is offered Communion under both species.

After Holy Communion, GIRM, 182, also notes that the deacon should immediately and reverently consume at the altar all the Blood of Christ that remains; he may be assisted by other deacons and priests in this ministerial task.

Further instructions are contained in GIRM, 183: "When the distribution of Communion is over, the Deacon returns to the altar with the Priest, collects the fragments, should any remain, and then carries the chalice and other sacred vessels to the credence table, where he purifies them and arranges them as usual, while the Priest returns to the chair. Nevertheless, it is also permitted to leave vessels needing to be purified on a corporal, suitably covered, on the credence table, and to purify them immediately after Mass, following the Dismissal of the people." Once the deacon leaves the credence table, he returns to his chair at the side of the Priest Celebrant.

It is important to note that *The Roman Missal* calls for a period of silence or a song of praise after Holy Communion. This gives people in the assembly some time to reflect on the life-giving gift they have just received from Christ.

The Prayer after Communion concludes the Communion Rite. The deacon may hold *The Roman Missal* for the celebrant. Note that parish announcements are not to be made before the Prayer after Communion.

Concluding Rites

These rites begins with parish announcements. The deacon makes these announcements unless the priest or another minister is assigned to do so. *The Roman Missal* also notes that any announcements are to be brief. Generally, try to avoid reading announcements that are carefully explained in the parish bulletin, thus delaying the conclusion of Mass.

The priest extends his hands for the greeting and dismissal and says, "The Lord be with you." The deacon responds with the people, his hands joined. GIRM, 185, notes that if a prayer over the people or a solemn formula for the blessing is used, the deacon says: "Bow down for the blessing."

After the dismissal, the deacon kisses the altar with the celebrant.

After the blessing, the deacon sends the people out into the world. He is to do so with hands joined. The words that the deacon speaks at the dismissal are prescribed by both the GIRM and *The Roman Missal*. GIRM, 185, notes that the deacon dismisses the people only by saying, "Go forth, the Mass is ended." On the other hand, *The Roman Missal* offers these additional options: "Go and announce the Gospel of the Lord" or "Go in peace, glorifying the Lord by your life" or "Go in peace."

After the dismissal, the deacon kisses the altar with the celebrant, moves around the altar and profoundly bows (or genuflects), then turns and processes out of the church. He walks on the right side and slightly ahead of the priest for the conclusion of Mass. If he is assisting the Bishop, the deacon may walk either a bit in front of or behind the Bishop so that the Bishop can be unimpeded as he blesses the people. Neither the *Book of the Gospels* nor the *Lectionary for Mass* is carried out at the end of Mass.

Sunday Celebrations in the Absence of a Priest

When a priest is not available to celebrate the Sunday Eucharist, the faithful may assemble in their own parish church for the celebration of the Liturgy of the Word with Holy Communion. The ritual book notes that as a minister of the word, who also has a special responsibility for the sacraments, the deacon is called in a special way to lead these Sunday assemblies. By virtue of his ordination, it belongs to him to lead the prayers, proclaim the Gospel, preach the homily, distribute Holy Communion, and give the final blessing and dismissal. He is always to be assisted by other liturgical ministers who normally participate in the celebration of Mass, including acolytes/altar servers, lectors or readers, cantors, Extraordinary Ministers of Holy Communion, and music ministers.

The deacon should use the ritual book, *Sunday Celebrations in the Absence of a Priest.* A Sunday Celebration in the Absence of a Priest may be Morning Prayer [with Holy Communion], Evening Prayer [with Holy Communion], or a Liturgy of the Word [with Holy Communion]. What follows is a celebration of the Liturgy of the Word [with Holy Communion.] Notice the bracketed [with Holy Communion.] Holy Communion is optional.

Introductory Rites

The Introductory Rites begin "without a procession." Once all have gathered instrumental music may be played. Then the deacon begins with the introduction that is included in the ritual book. This introduction sets the context for the importance of gathering on Sunday, even though Mass is not celebrated. This introduction is not done behind the altar or at the chair for the Priest Celebrant. Instead, the deacon stands in a "central place, facing the gathered assembly." The deacon continues with the Sign of the Cross and the Greeting. The Opening Prayer follows. The deacon may select from among the seasonal options that are provided in the ritual book.

Liturgy of the Word

The readings and psalms are those assigned in the *Lectionary for Mass* for that particular Sunday. Lectors, readers, and psalmists proclaim/ sing these words from the ambo as usual. Cantors sing the Gospel Acclamation. The deacon sits in the chair designated for his use (a chair other than that for the Priest Celebrant), listening and responding to God's word with the rest of the assembly.

Following a Gospel Acclamation, the deacon proclaims the Gospel from the ambo as is proper to his order; the reading is taken from the proper Sunday. Following the Gospel the deacon gives the homily. A period of silence takes place after the homily.

If catechumens are present, they may be dismissed after the period of silence. Next the deacon leads the assembly in the Profession of Faith. The Nicene Creed or Apostles' Creed may be used.

The deacon introduces and concludes the Prayer of the Faithful while another assisting minister announces the intentions. Two introductions to the Prayer of the Faithful are provided in the ritual as well as two conclusions to the prayer. Additional conclusions are found in Appendix III of the ritual. The petitions are found in Appendix I. If Holy Communion is not distributed, the service follows with an Act of Thanksgiving and the Concluding Rite (see below for a description of these elements).

Communion Rite

If Holy Communion is distributed, the deacon now goes to the tabernacle, "genuflects, takes the ciborium containing the body of the Lord, and places it on the altar."

From his chair, the deacon invites all to sing or recite the Lord's Prayer. Notice that the embolism and the doxology are omitted in the ritual.

The deacon then genuflects at the altar, takes a consecrated host, raises it slightly over the "vessel or ciborium, and facing the people, says: 'This is the Lamb of God . . . ,'" to which the assembly makes the usual response. The deacon then "reverently consumes the Body of Christ."

The deacon distributes Communion with other liturgical ministers, if they are needed. A song may be sung while the faithful are processing to receive Holy Communion. After Communion, the deacon returns the remaining hosts to the tabernacle and then returns to his chair. A period of silent prayer follows.

Then the deacon invites the faithful to stand for the Act of Thanksgiving. "This can be done by use of a psalm, a canticle, a hymn, a litany of praise, or a prayer." Five options are provided in the ritual as well as additional options in Appendix II of the ritual book. The deacon faces "the same direction as the gathered assembly" while he leads this prayer.

Concluding Rite

The Concluding Rite begins with announcements and the collection. The deacon then invites all to pray for vocations to the priesthood. The ritual provides text, but the deacon may use his own text as well. The deacon then says the final blessing and all are invited to offer the sign of peace. "A song, instrumental music or choral anthem of the day may conclude the celebration."

Liturgy of the Hours

In this public prayer of the universal Church, all the faithful (clergy, religious and lay people) praise God and sanctify the hours of the day. Whether this public ritual (liturgy) is celebrated in a cathedral filled with people or prayed by one person in a quiet room of their own house, it is the entire Church at worship. Thus it differs from other forms of prayer like the Rosary and Stations of the Cross, which may be prayed by a group of people but are private devotions.

Also known as the Divine Office, Liturgy of the Hours is a four-week cycle that consists of Morning and Evening Prayer, Daytime Prayer (or Midday), Night Prayer, and an Office of Readings. As clergy, deacons are obligated to pray the Liturgy of the Hours daily. In fact, deacons promise to do so during the Rite of Ordination. While deacons are encouraged to pray the Office at all hours (as priests are required to do), they are mandated (in the United States) to include at least Morning and Evening Prayer as part of their daily spiritual enrichment.

As reformed by Vatican II, the Liturgy of the Hours generally follows this structure: introductory prayers, hymn, two psalms and a canticle (from the Old Testament at Morning Prayer, the New Testament at Evening Prayer, with their antiphons (each psalm may be concluded by a prayer); scripture reading; responsory; Gospel canticle (either the Benedictus [Morning Prayer] or Magnificat [Evening Prayer]); intercessory prayers; a concluding blessing; and the dismissal.

Morning Prayer may begin with the invitatory (Psalm 95) if it is the first liturgical service of the day. Night Prayer generally consists of a hymn, one psalm, a short reading, Nunc Dimittis, prayer, and blessing.

Deacons are called in a particular way to preside at these liturgical celebrations. In fact, the National Directory notes that "whenever possible, [deacons] . . . should lead these prayers with the community to whom they have been assigned to minister."[12] When presiding, deacons must wear a stole over their alb; on greater solemnities, deacons may also wear a dalmatic. They also always wear a cincture. It belongs to the priest or deacon, at the chair, to greet the people, recite the introductory verse, begin the Lord's Prayer, say the concluding prayer, bless them, and dismiss them. Of course, deacons need to familiarize themselves with the Office itself, before leading prayer with an assembly. Such a review is beyond the scope of this book. However, the following briefly outlines the deacon's general role while presiding at simple Evening Prayer, usually prayed sometime between 4 PM and 7 PM. The assembly stands. The deacon simply starts at the chair or comes into the sanctuary and reverences the altar, then proceeds to the chair and, standing, opens the liturgy by making the Sign of the Cross and saying the introductory verse: "God, come to my assistance . . ." followed by the "Glory be . . ." (the doxology).

The hymn set the tone for the hour or feast day. When the hours are celebrated publicly, it is good practice to include a sung hymn, although the hymn can be chanted or read, too. After the hymn, all are seated.

The Psalmody follows—consisting of two psalms and a New Testament canticle (from the letters of the apostles or the book of Revelation) along with their associated antiphons. All pray the first antiphon, read the psalm, the doxology is prayed, the first antiphon is repeated, silence follows, and a psalm prayer is spoken. A deacon may want to divide the assembly into halves so that each takes turns reading or chanting individual psalm verses.

Repeat this same process for the second antiphon.

Again, repeat the process for the third antiphon, but note that a New Testament canticle will be used instead of a psalm.

A reading follows, and all continue to remain seated. The lector or reader should move to the ambo and proclaim the appropriate scripture reading. Note that the reading is not introduced as it is on Sunday ("A reading from . . ."), nor is it concluded with the phrase "The word of the Lord." It is simply proclaimed and followed with a period of silence.

A priest or deacon may offer a short homily.

A responsory follows; it can be prayed antiphonally.

The deacon stands with the rest of the assembly. He makes the Sign of the Cross as all pray the antiphon, recite the Canticle of Mary, pray the doxology, and repeat the canticle antiphon.

The deacon (and the assembly) continues to stand as they pray the intercessions. The intercessions lead directly into the Lord's Prayer, which is led by the deacon, who should make a brief invitation to pray ("Now let us pray as Christ taught us. Our Father . . ."). The concluding "Amen" is not spoken.

The deacon says the concluding prayer immediately after the Lord's Prayer without any introduction. Finally, prayer ends with the Sign of the Cross as the deacon gives the blessing and dismissal as is done at Mass: "The Lord be with you. . . . May almighty God bless you . . . . Go in peace."

Rite of Christian Initiation of Adults

Adults who inquire about the Catholic faith usually do so out of a prompting by the Holy Spirit. The process by which they may enter the Church was restored by the Second Vatican Council with the *Rite of Christian Initiation of Adults* (RCIA). This process has returned to its roots, reaching back to the early history of the Church; it is a path that allows inquirers and catechumens to reflect on their experiences of Death and Resurrection (in Christ) by sharing their own life journeys. The end result is that each catechumen can discover his/her own call to Baptism, Confirmation, and the Eucharist.

While Bishops are the chief stewards of the mysteries of God, and priests share in the teaching role of their Bishops, "deacons should be ready to assist in the ministry to catechumens . . . carrying out the steps, periods, and formation programs of the catechumenate wherever pastoral needs require."[13] What this means practically is that while presbyters preside at many liturgical rites of catechumens, deacons also may preside at several of these liturgical rites, in addition to presiding at the ritual scrutinies, presentations, and other minor rites.

Rite of Baptism for Children

Baptism is one of the Sacraments of Initiation (along with Confirmation and Eucharist) by which a person is incorporated into the life of Christ. *The Catechism of the Catholic Church* describes Baptism as a plunge into the waters symbolizing a person's burial into Christ's saving death "from which he rises up by resurrection with him as 'a new creature.' "[14] It is conferred by immersion or pouring of water while the Trinitarian formula is spoken by the minister: "I baptize you in the name of the Father, and of the Son, and of the Holy Spirit." The *Code of Canon Law* notes that the priest or deacon is the ordinary minister of Baptism, though lay persons may administer the sacrament under certain circumstances or in cases of dire necessity.

From the earliest times, the Church has baptized not only adults but children into the faith, a faith proclaimed for them by their parents and godparents who represent both the local Church, and all the saints and believers. The *Rite of Baptism for Children* notes that infants should be baptized "within the first weeks after birth."[15] In fact the introduction suggests that parents might contact their pastor for the baptismal arrangements even before the child is born!

Deacons typically are assigned by their pastors to preside at this liturgical ministry. Not only is he an ordinary minister of the sacrament

itself; he often collaborates with the pastor, associate pastors, other deacons and lay people in the
catechetical preparation of parents of infants/small
children (and adults through RCIA) who will
receive the sacrament. It is personally gratifying
for deacons not only to prepare a couple spiritually
for the gift of their child's Baptism, but to see the
fruition of that preparation come to pass by being
the presiding minister who welcomes the child into
the Church.

Deacons often perform many of the Baptisms in their assigned parishes.

Since deacons often perform many of the
Baptisms in their assigned parishes, it is important
that they understand and follow the ritual book. In
fact, the book itself exhorts that "all who perform
the rite of baptism should do so with exactness and
reverence; they must also try to be understanding and friendly to all."[16]
The second part of that instruction can be most challenging, especially
if the deacon is baptizing six crying babies at the same time while deal-
ing with late-arriving parents, sponsors, and family members, lack of
convenient parking, broken air conditioners or furnaces, etc. Perhaps
the best strategy for the deacon is simply to turn the celebration over to
God—and have a really good sense of humor!

Both deacons and the sacramental preparation teams should be
aware of the options presented in the ritual book for both the presiding
celebrant and the parents. He can use his own words to speak to the
parents at several points in the liturgical celebration as long as his
words theologically match the form and intent of the ritual text.
(While this is an option, I always strongly recommend that deacons
"Say the black, do the red," that is, use the words and follow the
instructions [norms and rubrics] of any sacramental/liturgical ritual
book.) Parents can choose from among several liturgical readings; of
course, the liturgical season may influence the readings chosen for the
Baptism, as well as color the homily of the deacon. The names of the
children to be baptized, and those of their brothers and sisters, may be
included in the invocation of the saints. There are even choices among
several final blessings. All these options serve to best meet the needs of
the families who present their children to the Lord.

Deacons also should remember that there are different ministries and roles in the celebration of Baptism. While he may be presiding at the sacrament, the mother and father will publicly ask the Church to baptize their child, mark their child with the Sign of the Cross, renounce Satan, recite the Profession of Faith, carry the child to the baptismal font, hold the lighted candle, and receive a special blessing at the end of the liturgy. Godparents also pledge to both help parents prepare for the Baptism, and assist them in Christian formation. Finally, members of the faith community witness and affirm the sacramental celebration.

Deacons who work with sacramental preparation teams in the parish's baptismal preparation ministry may find that these lay ministers will prepare the church for the Baptism. Even if they benefit from this generous ministry, deacons should run through their own sacramental checklist: Do you have a copy of the ritual book? Is the water clean and warm? Will a small pitcher or shell be used at the font for the pouring of the water, and is one ready? Do you have a towel to wipe the water from the baby's head? Are both the Oil of Catechumens and the Sacred Chrism readied? Do you have a towel to wipe the oil from your hands? Is the Paschal candle placed in the appropriate place for the Baptism? Is it lit? Have the white garment and baptismal candle been placed in their appropriate places for use during the rite? Have all the lights and the sound system been turned on? Do you have a lavaliere microphone if needed? Are the baptismal certificates completed correctly so that they can be presented to the parents after the Baptism?

Baptisms also are a great time for catechesis. Often, many family members and friends who have not attended church in years are excited to come to the baptismal liturgy. Be sure to generously welcome all with openness and affirmation. Before the sacrament begins, deacons should explain to the assembly gathered the movements through the church during the rite and what they signify. He should also take this opportunity to explain the main symbols used in the sacrament and their theological significance:

- Water—signifies our share in the Death and Resurrection of Christ.

- Chrism—indicates that the baptized share in the royal priesthood of Christ.

- White Garment—indicates the newly baptized has been clothed in Christ.

- Lighted Candle—the child has been enlightened by Christ, he or she now walks as a child of the light.

Additionally, this is a good time for a few "housekeeping" tasks as well. Have you asked the parents to open the baby's baptismal garment at the throat or breastbone so that you can anoint the infant without undue delay? This is especially important if a deacon is baptizing several babies at one liturgical celebration. Have you talked with younger children to be baptized (children 3–6 years old) in private but accompanied by their parents, and explained the liturgical actions you need to perform during the rite so that they understand what you will be doing as you approach them? Did you familiarize everyone with the layout of the church, including the rest rooms? Have you gone over ground rules for other small children present at the Baptism; discussed videos and photographer rules; and other special circumstances that can affect the required dignity of the celebration?

The actual Rite of Baptism for Children, which ordinarily takes place on Sunday, can be divided into four major movements: reception of the infants at the entrance of the Church; moving to the ambo for the proclamation of the word; bringing the baby to the baptismal font or pool, where the immersion or pouring of water will take place; and moving to the altar where prayers will be spoken and blessings given. Deacons might want to briefly explain the significance of the movements before the sacramental liturgy.

As deacons perform the rite, they want to ensure that all can actively participate in the liturgical celebration. Even though worship aids may be distributed, it is prudent for deacons to invite the assembly to sit or stand at various points in the rite, and to encourage their prayerful responses by announcing to the assembly what the expected response should be during various parts of the liturgy. For example, before the Prayer of the Faithful, deacons might share with the assembly, "Our response will be, 'Lord, hear our prayer.'"

Deacons also should be reminded that they represent the Church in a special way during these liturgies. Special care, then, should be taken to be patient, compassionate, and personal during the rite. It's always advisable to have a name "cheat sheet" handy just in case one suffers a "brain freeze" during the rite. (This can be most embarrassing when deacons preside at wake services, funerals, and interments . . . but that's for another book!)

Let us briefly move through the rite, assuming that the deacon is baptizing a single infant. And that while it is a Sunday celebration, the "communal setting" is an afternoon rather than during a Sunday parish Mass. This is more typical of most deacons' experiences.

Reception of the Child

The rite may start with a hymn or psalm suitable to the occasion. The deacon (vested in alb, cincture, or surplice, with a stole of festive color and with or without a cope) moves to the entrance of the church, where he greets the parents, godparents, and child to be baptized at the church door (but inside the vestibule). There he questions the parents about their intentions for the child, elicits the pledge of the parents' and godparents' regarding their responsibilities to raise the child in the faith, and claims the child for Christ by signing him or her on the forehead with the Sign of the Cross. He invites the parents and godparents to mark the child as well. Then he welcomes all into the church to take part in the Liturgy of the Word, processing to a place near the ambo; Psalm 84 or another suitable hymn can be sung during this procession. (Deacons should note that if several children are to be baptized at the same liturgy, those children may be carried or led to a separate place at this time [like a crying room, or even outside the main church] where they remain until the end of the Liturgy of the Word.)

The Liturgy of the Word is proclaimed at the ambo. Old and New Testament readings, including psalms, are selected from many options in the ritual book in collaboration with parents, and may be proclaimed by lay ministers, if present. However, proclamation of any Gospel reading is the ministry of the ordained alone. Therefore it is important for deacons to remember that if Baptismal preparation ministers— or even the deacon's wife—are part of the liturgical team who perform specific ministries during the rite, the proclamation of the Gospel belongs to the deacon.

After the readings, the celebrant offers a short homily. It is a wonderful opportunity for the deacon to explain that spiritual rebirth is a precious gift from God, initiating one into God's own life, and into membership of the faith community. It also is an appropriate time to speak of the parents' and godparents' duties as Christian role models, and to broaden that call by inviting all to the responsibility of helping the child during his/her life to grow in faith and become rich in the grace that Jesus offers to all of us. All deacons should understand that the homily can be a potent instrument for evangelization for inactive Catholics or members of other Christian religious denominations. Therefore the words spoken and the demeanor taken by the deacon during the homily—already inspired by the Holy Spirit—can possibly be used by the Holy Spirit to open one's heart again (or for the first time) to the Lord. Be welcoming, compassionate, and compelling in a spirit of generosity and humility. A suitable hymn may follow the homily.

The Liturgy of the Word continues with the Prayer of the Faithful and the invocation of saints. In additional to those contained in the rite, the ritual book also offers other forms for general intercessions and suggestions for the invocation. Again, these may be chosen in collaboration with the parents of the child to be baptized. (Deacons should note that when several children are being baptized and have been taken out of church during the Liturgy of the Word, they should return before the invocation of the saints.)

The Prayer of Exorcism and Anointing immediately follows. It may be wise to relieve the anxiety of both parents and other participants by explaining that this "exorcism" is not like ones they might have seen in movies, but rather a prayer that seeks to free and protect the child from the evils of sin and temptation. After the prayer, the deacon anoints the child with the Oil of Catechumens on the breast. Deacons should note that the ritual book explains the anointing may be omitted only when the minister of Baptism judges the occasion to be pastorally necessary or desirable. In my experience, I have never had the occasion to omit the anointing—even when I had 20 children to baptize at one liturgical celebration. However, if a deacon were to skip the anointing, he would say the alternate words provided in the rite, and lay his hand on the child in silence.

Now the deacon may invite the child, parents, and godparents to the baptistery or font, where he proceeds with the blessing and invocation of God over baptismal water. Using one of the formulas provided by the rite, the deacon recalls God's blessing on water during epochs in our faith history, and then asks the Father, with the Son, to send the Holy Spirit upon the water of the font. While he does this, his right hand should be touching the water itself.

At the Renunciation of Sin and Profession of Faith, the deacon speaks directly to parents and godparents, asking them through one of the formulae provided to renounce sin and profess their faith. Upon completion, the entire assembly gives their assent to this Profession of Faith just witnessed by responding "Amen" to the deacon's words: "This is our faith. This is the faith of the Church. We are proud to profess it, in Christ Jesus our Lord."

Now comes the actual Rite of Baptism. The deacon invites the immediate family to gather closely around the font. If the Baptism is to be performed by infusion (pouring), the rite notes that it is preferable that the mother hold the child. It does allow the father to hold the child, but since the title "father" is included in parentheses only, clearly the intention is for the mother to take up this duty. In places where it is the long-ingrained custom for the godmother (or godfather) to hold the child, this is permissible. In the case of immersion, the mother or father or either godparent may lift the child out of the baptismal pool.

Before the deacon immerses or pours water, he should ensure that the immediate family is gathered around the font so that all can see and/or participate in the sacrament. Once you have the immediate family around the baptismal font or pool, you might consider inviting the rest of the family (especially grandparents) and friends of the family to come forward and gather around the font, if practicable.

Since this is a benchmark event in the faith life of a Catholic family, videos and photographs of the Baptism can become important icons. Give some time for camera wielders to get in place before the Baptism occurs, while being considerate to the viewing space of others.

Deacons (and priests) must only use the prescribed Trinitarian formula for Baptism, that is, "[Name of child], 'I baptize you in the name of the Father, and of the Son, and of the Holy Spirit,'" immersing or pouring water upon the child or immersing the child after each phrase. It is not acceptable to use other words, such as, "I baptize you in the name of the Creator, the Redeemer, and the Sanctifier." That would certainly constitute an invalid Baptism.

When using the infusion method for Baptism, the deacon should pour a generous amount of water over the head (forehead) of the child after each phrase of the Baptismal formula. When using the immersion method for Baptism (in an immersion pool), a deacon may immerse the baby in water up to its neck, and then pour a good amount of water over the baby's head. You can ask for assistance in placing the baby into the water, that is, ask the mother to hold the child in that position so you can be free to pour and speak the words of Baptism.

Be sure to have dry towels for the baby when using either method; for immersion, you might even consider setting up the crying room with a padded table to lay the child and dry him or her off before continuing the rite.

The Explanatory Rites follow the immersion or pouring of water. First, the deacon speaks a prayer, then anoints the child on the crown of the head (not the forehead!) with Sacred Chrism. A lavish amount of chrism should be used, and it should not be wiped off the baby's head.

Another prayer precedes the clothing with the white garment. It is good to have the parents provide a special white garment that could be used for subsequent Baptisms in the family. Of course, the child, in all likelihood, will be wearing a white baptismal gown for the Baptism.

Next comes the presentation of the lighted candle. The rite says, "The celebrant takes the Easter candle and says . . . ."[17] This immediately presents a problem in most parishes since the Paschal candle is quite large and set firmly in an often ornate candle stand. More practical, the celebrant can take the unlighted baptismal candle that will be handed to the parents or godparents, light it himself from the Paschal candle, and hand it over. Or the deacon might have one of the parents or godparents light the candle from the Paschal candle themselves. But then one needs to be concerned about safety questions, such as, "Can someone reach the Paschal candle? Do you need a step stool to reach the candle? Is the stool stable?"

One additional suggestion related to the candle: At the end of the entire ritual, as part of your closing thank you's and remarks, the deacon might invite the parents to light the baptismal candle on other benchmark days in the child's life as a remembrance of and connection to their Baptism; these might include birthdays, saint-name days, first day of school, first Reconciliation, First Holy Communion, and so on.

The Rite of Ephphetha (or prayer over the ears and mouth) follows, although in the United States the ritual book notes that it may be performed at the discretion of the minister.[18] Unless there is a serious health or cultural issue involved, celebrants are not to skip this action of the Baptismal rite. Deacons should recall the powerful symbolism and theology behind this ritual action. In Mark 7:31–37, Jesus heals a deaf man who had a speech impediment by putting his finger into the man's ears, and by spitting and touching the man's tongue. The he said, "Ephphatha!" ("Be opened!") And immediately the man's ears were opened and his speech impediment was removed. As the *Rite of Christian Initiation of Adults* (Preparation Rites on Holy Saturday) tells us, the powerful symbolism of this action impresses on the elect (or in the case of infant Baptism, the parents, godparents, family, and so on) the need for God's generous grace in order that they may hear the word of God clearly and profess it for their salvation.[19] So this is a powerful cat-echetical reminder that the parents and godparents have pledged to do all in their power to raise the newly baptized child in a faith-centered family which will foster in him or her a greater awareness of God's gra-cious presence in their lives. (Of course, deacons might explain this rite as part of the "symbols" review prior to the start of the liturgy.)

At the conclusion of the rite, there is a procession to the altar. The lighted baptismal candle is carried in the procession. The deacon addresses the entire assembly and leads them in singing or saying the Lord's Prayer. Deacons may recall that this movement is so important because it makes the connection between the child's Baptism and the Sacrament of the Eucharist; since Baptism is the doorway or gate to all the other sacraments, it should eventually lead the newly baptized to the Eucharistic table.

The blessing and dismissal conclude the rite. The deacon first blesses the mother while she holds the child in her arms, then the father, and lastly the entire assembly. Be aware of the different options for the prayer; this allows deacons to be sensitive to the situation regarding the presence of one or both parents at the Baptism.

A suitable hymn can follow. As the ritual book notes, if there is a custom or practice of bringing the newly baptized child to the altar of our Blessed Mother after the rite, it should be done at this time.

Outside of the ritual and as part of your thank-you words, invite family and friends to come into the sanctuary for photographs and videos, if they wish (and if your local parish church allows it). Don't

remove your alb, cincture, and stole anytime soon, either; most celebrants will be asked to pose for pictures with the baptized child, parents and family.

After parting words and photos, the deacon still has work to do.
My suggestion is to sign the baptismal certificates only after the
Baptism has taken place; be certain that the parish's embossed seal is
affixed to this important document. Do the same for godparents' certificates, if used. The box for the child's baptismal candle with all the
pertinent information written on its side also should be presented to
the parents. You also should ensure that the sacred oils are returned to
their rightful place (in the ambry or other secure location). Empty into
the sacrarium the unused water blessed for the Baptism and clean the
bowl. And perform other "cleanup" chores that ready the church for its
next celebration.

Finally, I suggest that deacons model the parish's hospitality and
welcome of a new member into its family by doing what ministers do at
the end of any liturgy: Stay in the church, vested, near the main
entrance or the entrance from which most of the assembly will leave
the church, and shake hands, chat, and thank all for attending the
Baptism. This small gesture not only is appreciated by families, but
often (at least in my experience) creates an opportunity for attendees to
speak with a cleric about "church," and their own experiences.

Essentially, it is a wonderful opportunity for evangelization! One
final note is necessary as a reminder to deacons. The *Rite of Baptism for
Children* notes that the term "children" or "infants" refer to those who
have not yet reached the age of discernment and therefore cannot profess personal faith for themselves.[20] In the United States, the Bishops
have determined that the age of reason is seven years old. This means
that any child under the age of seven may be baptized by a priest or
deacon using this rite.

However, its corollary also mandates that children seven and older
(that is, of catechetical age) are initiated by using the *Rite of Christian
Initiation of Adults*. The rite may be adapted to better suit the needs of
children. But deacons should understand that there is no official Rite of
Christian Initiation of Children (RCIC). That name is simply a term
(incorrectly) adapted by some parishes to indicate that they offer a children's catechetical program.

Rite of Confirmation

The Sacrament of Confirmation, which is the special gift of the Holy Spirit promised by Christ and first poured out on his Church (the apostles) at Pentecost, is conferred through the anointing with chrism on the forehead, by the laying on of the Bishop's (celebrant's) hands, and through the words "Be sealed with the gift of the Holy Spirit." In the Latin rite, the ordinary minister of Confirmation is the Bishop. In cases of necessity, the Bishop may grant the faculty of administering the sacrament to priests. In danger of death, any priest may administer Confirmation to a Christian.

However, the deacon often plays a role in both the preparation for and the liturgical celebration of Confirmation. Deacons, by virtue of their threefold ordained ministry of service to the word, liturgy, and charity, share in the responsibility of the pastor and other catechists to "see that all the baptized reach the completion of Christian initiation . . ."[21] Typically, deacons at their assigned parishes may teach in religious education classes, sacramental preparation classes, and the Rite of Christian Initiation of Adults sessions that focus on Confirmation. Part of the deacon's responsibility in these classes is to ensure that the participants understand how the Holy Spirit is alive in their lives, and to gradually accept that with the sacrament comes an obligation to practice an active faith that includes frequent reception of the sacraments, regular Mass attendance, a vibrant prayer life, and a willingness to witness Christ's love and compassion to the world. For a deacon who has prepared those who receive Confirmation at a special liturgy or during the Easter Vigil, his presence can be very powerful for the *confirmandi*; it also can maintain the connection he has made with them during classes, and help to strengthen his pastoral relationship with them as they put their faith into action.

Even if a deacon has not participated in the preparation of those being formed for Confirmation, he ordinarily participates in the parish's liturgical celebration of the sacrament. Assisting the Bishop and the pastor at this liturgy expresses for the assembly the fullness of Holy Orders present on the altar; it's also incumbent of the deacon that he exercises his service to the Liturgy.

The Sacrament of Confirmation is ordinarily celebrated at Mass. Deacons who assist at these liturgies perform all their typical Mass duties and responsibilities. There also are some additional tasks that he may perform.

However, even though a sacristan or sacramental preparation team may be working in collaboration with the deacon, the deacon should remember that his office makes him the Bishop's (and concelebrants') primary assistant for this liturgy. This means that the deacon should take care that the special items necessary for the celebration of the sacrament are prepared. These include matching vestments for the Bishop, concelebrants, and deacon, if possible. If this cannot be done, the deacon should nevertheless wear a dalmatic; a sufficient number of chairs placed in the sanctuary for the Bishop, concelebrants, deacon(s), and other liturgical ministers. Even with the pastor and other concelebrants, the deacon as the Bishop's (celebrant's) primary assistant sits on the Bishop's right, even with the presence of priest concelebrants; a vessel (or several vessels) to hold the Sacred Chrism; a pitcher of warm, soapy water, bowl and towels for the Bishop to wipe chrism from his hands; and provide wedges of lemon on a plate next to the water bowl (it helps to remove the chrism after anointing). Ensure that the *Rite of Confirmation* is in its proper place and that there are enough hosts and wine so that Holy Communion can be distributed to the assembly under both species.

During the liturgy, deacons assume their regular ministries. However, there are some additional responsibilities for the deacon when a Bishop is present. In the absence of acolytes or altar servers, the deacon may be required to assist the Bishop with his miter and pastoral staff during the liturgy. The *Ceremonial of Bishops*, 59 notes, "As a rule, the bishop holds the pastoral staff, its curved head turned away from himself and toward the people."

After his proclamation of the Gospel, the deacon usually does not reverence the *Book of the Gospels* with a kiss, but instead solemnly carries the book to the Bishop so that he may venerate it, or use it for a special blessing. (Check with either the Master of Ceremonies or the Bishop, himself, before the liturgy begins, to know his preference.) In either case, the deacon then places the book on the credence table or in a suitable place.

The presentation of the candidates takes place before the Bishop begins his homily. Usually, the candidates simply stand in place, according to the custom of the region. If there is a large number of candidates for Confirmation (for example, more than 100), you may present the Confirmation class as a whole to the Bishop without calling out the individual names. If there is a smaller group to be confirmed, then all the names of the candidates for Confirmation are read. Please consult with the Bishop's Master of Ceremonies or the Bishop's office to see if the Bishop prefers not to call all the candidates by name when there is a large number of candidates to confirm.

After the laying on of hands by the Bishop and priests, the deacon brings the Sacred Chrism to the Bishop for the anointing. Some pastors prefer to hold the chrism during the anointing. In that case, the deacon often is asked to hold the Bishop's pastoral staff during this time, standing to his immediate left while the pastor with chrism stands on the Bishop's immediate right. Other times, the associate pastor is asked to hold the crosier during the anointing; then the deacon should either return to his chair or stand attentively near the credence table in case there is some need for his assistance.

If the deacon does hold the chrism for the Bishop during the anointing, he should hold it so that the Bishop can elegantly and reverently dip his thumb into the sacred oil to anoint the foreheads of the confirmation candidates. At the conclusion of the anointing, the deacon should return the chrism to the credence table or special place that had been prepared for it in the sanctuary. He also should assist the Bishop in the washing of his hands. Occasionally, a Bishop will wish to wash his hands at the chair; in that case, the deacon (if alone) brings a tray with the prepared items on it. In any case, the deacon should be attentive to the Bishop's needs. Once the rite is completed, all return to their chairs.

The rite calls for the "deacon or minister" to announce the Prayer of the Faithful. The Prayer of the Faithful is part of the ministry of the deacon at any liturgy. However, sometimes the pastor has given permission for some of the *confirmandi* to announce the intentions. If that is the case, deacons should work collaboratively with the *confirmandi* to ensure that the intentions are announced with the dignity they deserve.

A Solemn Blessing is offered at the end of the rite. As before all Solemn Blessings, the deacon gives the invitation to the assembly. After the blessing, the deacon would dismiss the assembly as usual.

Finally, for the procession at the end of Mass, the deacon walks with the Bishop, either a bit in front of him or behind him, to give the Bishop sufficient room to offer his blessing to the assembly.

Rite of Penance

Deacons are not ordinary ministers of the Sacrament of Penance. Canon Law expressly notes that it is priests alone who can offer sacramental absolution for sins; of course, they must have the faculty to absolve sins in accordance with canon law. However, deacons can assist priests in communal rites of reconciliation by proclaiming the Gospel, preaching the homily, leading the assembly into a reflective examination of conscience, instructing the assembly to bow their heads for the final blessing, and dismissing them.

However, deacons may preside at non-sacramental reconciliation services offered at the parish to prepare individuals for reception of the sacrament from a priest. These non-sacramental penitential celebrations are essentially the same as a celebration of the word and follow a specific structure: introductory rites (song, greeting, and prayer); one or more biblical readings; psalms or periods of silence between them; homily; a communal prayer or litany; recitation of the Lord's Prayer, closing prayer, and dismissal (which includes a blessing).

Deacons should note the ritual book cautions that care should be taken so the faithful do not confuse these reconciliation or penitential services with the celebration of the Sacrament of Penance. Therefore, deacons must remind the assembly of this fact, and encourage them to receive sacramental confession and absolution, itself.

The rite also provides three sample penitential celebrations in Appendix II (Advent and Lent), as well as offering common themes for such services.

Finally, the rite notes that these penitential celebration models "should be adapted to the specific conditions and needs of each community."[22] While this gives deacons certain freedoms in preparing these celebrations, it does not allow them to alter the mandated structure of the service or otherwise stray from the norms.

Rite of Marriage

Deacons would be wise to remember, and remind brides and grooms, that the marriage of two Catholic Christians is at the same time a personal and an ecclesial event. The wedding liturgy, either within or outside of Mass, is a sacramental encounter with Christ in the midst of the faithful. During the liturgy, all give thanks and praise to our God who manifests his loving presence in the marriage covenant of a particular couple. So it is more than the bride's special day or the groom's special day—it is a special day for the entire Church!

Deacons may be the Church's official witness when two people administer the sacrament of Marriage to each other; however, they must receive that delegation, as must priests, from the local pastor. But long before the rite, itself, deacons often work with engaged couples to prepare for their sacramental marriages.

Deacons may conduct the prenuptial interviews at the parish with the bride and groom, completing the prenuptial questionnaire forms that ascertain freedom and readiness to enter into the sacrament, as well as documenting the couple's marriage preparation program certificate (PreCana, etc.). While this interview requires much pastoral skill and sensitivity, the particulars of the interview are beyond the scope of this book. General objectives for these interviews might be helpful: To establish a comfortable relationship with the couple, getting to know them as they get to know you; discover sooner rather than later any sacramental impediments or serious complications to the relationship; to get paperwork and required documentation into your hands as soon as possible; help the couple understand their need to communicate their needs regarding the wedding liturgy to each other and to you; enhance the couple's awareness about the sacramental covenant in the sacrament of Marriage; learn the status of their faith life as well as their families' faith life; get to know their concerns about the wedding and help them when possible; let them know up front all that is required of them (both canonically and at your parish). It is best that deacons give the couple both the diocese's and parish's marriage preparation booklet at the first meeting.

There is additional paperwork involved as couples prepare for the marriage. Needed are copies of their baptismal certificates, dated within six months of the wedding date and marked with the seal of the

Church that administered them; these certificates also should contain the date of their reception of Holy Communion and Confirmation. (While the reception of Confirmation is often mandated by certain pastors, it is not absolutely required for a Catholic marriage.) Also needed are witness affidavits, and a civil marriage license.

Additional documentation may be necessary; it could include: canonical permissions or dispensations, with their own required documents; annulment papers; interfaith consent form; written permission for minors from parents and vicar; permission of proper pastor for a marriage in a parish not that of a bride or groom; and for widows or widowers, both a marriage certificate of the previous marriage and a death certificate of the deceased spouse.

Deacons themselves may need certain documents such as delegation to the proper pastor for an officiating deacon not assigned to the parish where the marriage is taking place; and a temporary solemniser form for a deacon's temporary state approval to witness a marriage in a state other than that of his residence. Most dioceses have a priest appointed at the Pastoral Center (Chancery Office) who helps extern priests obtain the necessary approval to celebrate a wedding on a particular occasion in their diocese. It is best to check with this person to clarify the procedures followed in this diocese.

Once deacons have completed these steps and reviewed all required paperwork with the engaged couple, then they are ready to guide the bride and groom through a review of the Rite of Marriage, and help them prepare the entire liturgy.

The *Rite of Marriage*, which contains the prayers, readings, and liturgical options used for Catholic weddings, provides engaged couples with both structure and choices. There are three forms for the Rite of Marriage: within Mass when two Catholics marry; outside of Mass, usually used when a Catholic marries a person from another Christian denomination; and outside of Mass, for Catholics marrying someone who is not baptized. Deacons more commonly preside at weddings outside of Mass, although they sometimes are asked to assist at a wedding Mass and perform the Rite of Marriage within the Mass. What follows is an examination of the rite outside Mass.

Introductory Rites

Deacons, wearing their alb, cincture, and stole (and white cope, if desired), may greet the bride and groom at the door of the church or at the altar. If there is a procession, the other liturgical ministers go first, followed by the deacon, the bridal party, and then the bride and groom. Sometimes, the groom is the first person in the procession after the liturgical ministers, leaving the end of the procession for the bride and person(s) accompanying her down the aisle. They may be accompanied by "at least their parents and two witnesses."[23] (It is beyond the scope of this book to describe all the different forms of entrance for the bride, groom, and wedding party, as well as their locus near the altar or in the pews.)

Deacons should note that the music for the procession can be instrumental, but the rite has a preference for the music to be sung by the assembly. Also note that secular music is an inappropriate choice for wedding liturgies (even if it speaks of love, God, or is the bride's favorite song). The choice of music should encourage the full, conscious, and active participation of the entire assembly; it also should reflect with reverence the sacramental purpose of the liturgy.

The deacon should greet the assembly, expressing the Church's joy over the celebration taking place. He might follow the greeting by a prayer, or move directly to the Liturgy of the Word.

Liturgy of the Word

Readings at Catholic weddings are a proclamation of God's word, and of the Church's teachings about faith and the sacrament of Marriage. For this reason, readings are limited to choices from scripture only. No other texts, including poems or reflections, may substitute for these readings. There are nine options for the First Reading, thirteen options for the Second Reading, and ten options for the Gospel. A couple can choose to have only two readings proclaimed; however, one must be from the Gospel. Also, a Responsorial Psalm should be included between the First and Second Readings (if three are chosen) per usual. Deacons should ensure that the word is proclaimed reverently; it is a desirable practice that reader(s) chosen by the engaged couple be readers in their home parishes; if they are not, special care should be taken at the rehearsal so that the readers can proclaim the word in an appropriate manner to the assembly.

The deacon proclaims the Gospel; his homily should speak to the mystery of Christian marriage, dignity of wedded love, grace of the sacrament, and responsibilities of married people. His challenge is in writing a homily that explains all the above in simple everyday language that relates to the particulars of the couple and their families.

Rite of Marriage

The actual Rite of Marriage includes several elements that should be conducted with reverence and dignity by the deacon. Note that the ritual book calls for all to stand during the rite.[24]

Questions: After some preliminary words, the deacon questions the couple about their freedom to choose marriage, their love for each other, and their openness to accept the blessing of children in their marriage.

Consent: The deacon asks the couple to declare publicly their consent to marry each other. They should join hands and turn toward each other to do so. This consent is commonly referred to as the "marriage vows." The couple may choose an option from the rite, and whether they would like to speak the vows to each other or have the deacon receive their consent by questioning them. After their "vows," the deacon assents to the couple's consent in the name of the Church.

One brief note: Sometimes a couple is disappointed to learn that they cannot write their own vows. Deacons might encourage the couple to include their own personal pledges of love and fidelity in the printed wedding program instead.

Blessing and the exchange of rings: First the deacon blesses the rings with the Sign of the Cross, then the couple places the rings on each other's ring fingers while saying the prescribed words. (To avoid confusion or delay here, the deacon should have made certain before the liturgy that the rings to be blessed and exchanged were being held by a designated person. We've all seen groomsmen frantically searching their persons for rings that they thought were in their pockets!)

Prayer of the Faithful: The Prayer of the Faithful takes place after the deacon speaks an introduction to the blessing of the couple. This introduction could be followed by a brief silence; then petitions are offered. Intercessions are not included in the rite. Deacons should write (or collaborate with the couple) these intercessions based on the rubrical formula designated in GIRM, 69 and 70. These petitions may include several special intentions of the couple, including family members.

Nuptial Blessing: This is a special blessing for the bride and groom, and not to be confused with the general blessing of the entire assembly which follows the Lord's Prayer. The deacon, with hands joined, introduces the blessing with the prescribed words (depending on the Nuptial Blessing chosen by the couple); then he extends his hands and continues with the blessing.

Conclusion of the Celebration

The recitation of the Lord's Prayer, and the final blessing ends the liturgy. Since the rite does not prescribe a closing procession, the deacon and other ministers may remain at the altar while the bride and groom leave together as husband and wife.

Important note: The rite does allow Holy Communion to be distributed to the assembly in a liturgy outside Mass. Article 54 of the rite seems to suggest that if a Mass was requested but the church was unable to accommodate this request because no priest was available, then Holy Communion might be offered. Check with your diocesan office about guidelines or policies concerning Communion services being added to wedding ceremonies.

Pastoral Care of the Sick

The Church witnesses to the life of the faithful through the pastoral care of the sick and infirm by the service of Bishops, priests, deacons, consecrated religious, and lay pastoral ministers. In fact, taking care of those who suffer from infirmities is one of the most significant ways we, as the body of Christ, participate in the mission and ministry of Jesus.

Pastoral Care of the Sick: Rites of Anointing and Viaticum offers instructions as to how these rites should be conducted. While only priests can offer the Sacrament of the Anointing of the Sick to those who are ill, deacons may deliver the Holy Communion to the sick and administer Viaticum to the dying. They should follow the norms and rubrics of the ritual book when they do so. Deacons also may visit hospitals, nursing and assisted living homes, and homes, provided they have been competently trained for these ministries.

When the Sacrament of the Anointing of the Sick is offered within a Mass, the deacon may assist at the liturgy as usual. Deacons may preach the homily, ensuring that they explain both how the sacred texts speak to the meaning of illness in the Paschal Mystery, and of the graces given by the sacrament.

They may hold the book for the priest during prayers and when oil is being blessed (or thanksgiving is being offered for oil already blessed).

They may accompany the priest while he is in the act of anointing each of the sick, holding the vessel containing the oil. It also is helpful for deacons to carry a small card with the printed words of the anointing for easy reference during the ritual.

Upon completion of the anointing, the deacon may assist the priest with the washing of his hands, being certain to have prepared prior to the liturgy a pitcher of warm soapy water, water bowl, quartered lemon, and towel.

As during any Mass, the deacon should pay particular attention to those sick or disabled who need special attention during the reception of Holy Communion.

If the anointing takes place outside the Mass, deacons may proclaim the Gospel, preach the homily, assist the priest by holding the book during the prayers, holding the sacred oil during the actual anointing, assist with the washing of the priest's hands after the anointing, and help distribute Holy Communion to the gathered assembly.

Order of Christian Funerals

As the ritual book notes, in the face of death, the Church confidently proclaims that God has created each person for eternal life, and that by his Death and Resurrection, Jesus has destroyed death forever. Therefore Christians celebrate funeral rites to offer worship, praise, and thanksgiving for the gift of life which has been returned to its Creator.

We also pray that those who have died receive forgiveness for their sins and the gift of everlasting life.

The *Order for Christian Funerals* (OCF) tells us that when no priest is available, deacons, as ministers of the word, altar, and of charity, preside at funeral rites. Therefore deacons may preside at wake services, funeral services outside of Mass, and at the cemetery interment; they may also assist at the funeral Mass. They should understand fully the norms and rubrics for these celebrations, be familiar with the sacred texts offered as options, and understand the intrinsic unity of these elements of Christian funerals as they preside at these prayerful gatherings. At all times, deacons should remember that the ministry of the Church during these often stressful times is one of gently accompanying mourners, affirming the love and compassion of Jesus and his promise of eternal life.

The main rites of the OCF are the Vigil for the Deceased, Funeral Mass or funeral liturgy outside of Mass, and the Rite of Committal.

Vigil for the Deceased

This rite (more commonly referred to as a wake service) may be celebrated by the Christian community, and led by a deacon in the parish church before the funeral liturgy, at a funeral home, in the home of the deceased, or another suitable place. It is an important moment in the Christian community's public prayer for the deceased. The vigil in the form of the Liturgy of the Word consists of: the Introductory Rites, the Liturgy of the Word with homily, prayers of intercession, and a Concluding Rite. While norms and rubrics for the rite are contained in the ritual book, deacons should note that the ritual calls for the encouragement by the minister for the full participation of all present, as well as encouraging family members to assume some liturgical roles (unless their grief prevents them from doing so). The rite also notes that music is integral to any vigil; so deacons should collaborate with their parish's music ministers to choose, in consultation with the families, appropriate music for the liturgy, and to provide an organist, instrumentalist, or cantor.

Deacons should consult with families, when possible, in choosing prayers, readings, and music for the vigil service. When celebrating the official liturgy of the Church, deacons must always wear the proper vestments. This includes services at funeral homes.

Families may choose to print (in collaboration with the deacon and/or funeral director) an order of service or worship aid for the vigil celebration; besides prayers, music and blessings, the booklet might include a photograph of the deceased and some biographical information. If this is not done, the funeral home often provides booklets of the Vigil text for use by the mourners.

Deacons should note that the vigil, not the funeral liturgy, is the proper place for a member of the family or friend of the deceased to speak an eulogy in remembrance of the deceased. The rite calls for this to take place after the prayer of intercession and before the blessing, or at some other suitable time during the vigil (for example, after the deacon's homily). In addition, offering the eulogy at the vigil is more sensitive to grieving families who may find it difficult to sit through an unnecessarily prolonged Mass that included several testimonies for the deceased. (Be sure to check with your diocese to learn of its policy regarding the OCF and eulogies.)

While the formal vigil ritual is often the preferred rite for the deceased before the funeral liturgy, some families may prefer a simple recitation of the Rosary. If a deacon is asked to pray the Rosary, note that he has much freedom in structuring the rite: He may lead a simple recitation of three Our Fathers, three Hail Mary's, and a Glory Be, in addition to a blessing; he may recite a decade or an entire Rosary; or he may include with the Rosary a few hymns, scripture readings, prayer of intercession, eulogy, and a blessing.

Funeral Liturgy (within or outside Mass)

At the funeral liturgy, as the ritual book notes, the community gathers with the family and friends of the deceased to give praise and thanks to God for Christ's victory over death, to commend the deceased to God's tender mercy and compassion, and to seek strength in the proclamation of the Paschal Mystery. When a member of the faith community dies, deacons (and priests) should encourage that this celebration take place within the Mass. When Mass cannot be celebrated or the family requests otherwise (for example, many of the mourners may not be

Catholic or have ceased to practice the faith), the liturgy is celebrated outside of Mass.

During Mass, deacons perform the regular duties of their office during the funeral liturgy, including the possibly of preaching the homily; but they should also be familiar with additional movements of the rite and adaptations of the liturgy. For example, for the reception of the body at the beginning of Mass, the deacon accompanies the celebrant and other ministers to the door of the church and takes his place next to the priest. He may hand the pall and holy water sprinkler to the priest (unless altar servers do so). He can invite the assembly to turn toward the casket to participate in the reception rite. Then when the body is placed before the altar, he bows and reverences the altar with the priest, and proceeds to his chair for the Collect. He may need to hold *The Roman Missal* for the celebrant if no altar servers are present.

Although no special movements or adaptations take place during the Liturgy of the Word, the deacon may be called to assist the priest with the boat and thurible if incense is used during the preparation of the gifts. In this case, before the washing of hands, he would help the celebrant place incense in the thurible, and accompany the priest as he blesses the gifts and altar. Afterward, the deacon may incense the priest and congregation.

Following the Prayer after Communion, the deacon may make any necessary announcements about the committal service at the cemetery or luncheon arrangements. Then he accompanies the priest to a place near the casket for the Final Commendation. If no other ministers are present, the deacon may carry the thurible and holy water. (Note that if the body was sprinkled with holy water at the rite of reception during the beginning of the Mass, it is ordinarily omitted here.)

Then the deacon will accompany the priest with other ministers in procession to the back of the church. As this procession begins, the deacon says, "In peace let us take N. to his /her place of rest." Then he stands with the priest while the casket is prepared for the journey to the cemetery.

Funeral Liturgy outside Mass

There are two primary differences for deacons at this liturgy: they preside, and the Liturgy of the Word has a different structure.

As presider, deacons should give great care to their words, gestures, and prayers which affect the assembly's emotional as well as spiritual well-being. They must show reverence for the body as a temple of the Holy Spirit, and provide an atmosphere of sensitive concern and confident faith. They must also give great witness to what it means to be part of the body of Christ and a caring community of faith.

During the Liturgy of the Word, the usual structure of readings, homily, and Prayer of the Faithful is followed by the Lord's Prayer. The celebration also may include Holy Communion. If distributed, the deacon goes to the tabernacle to bring reserved hosts to the altar. Then he invites the faithful to Holy Communion by leading the Lamb of God, and distributes the body of Christ in the usual way. After all have received Communion, the deacon returns the unused consecrated hosts to the tabernacle, and then says one of the prescribed Prayers after Communion. Finally, he concludes the funeral liturgy in the usual way.

Rite of Committal

This rite "can help the mourners face the end of one relationship with the deceased and to begin a new one based on prayerful remembrance, gratitude, and the hope of resurrection and reunion."[25] Yet most deacons discover that the committal is either a joyous final celebration or a very sorrowful parting. Either way, it is a stark and powerful expression of final separation in this life.

The short and simple rite may be celebrated at the grave, cemetery chapel, crematorium, and may be used at sea. Deacons may preside over the rite; they should vest according to local custom. This usually means in an alb, cincture, and stole of proper color for the celebration. The general structure of the rite is an invitation, scripture verse, prayer over the place of committal, committal, intercessions, the Lord's Prayer, concluding prayer, and Prayer over the People, which includes a blessing. A song may conclude the rite. If the Rite of Committal with Final Commendation is used, the deacon may sprinkle the casket with holy water after the invitation to prayer or during the Song of Farewell.

At the conclusion of either ritual, and if it is the local custom, an appropriate gesture of farewell may be offered by family and friends. This can include placing flowers on the casket to sprinkling the coffin with holy water. If people choose the latter, deacons should assist them with the aspergillum (holy water sprinkler).

Book of Blessings

Blessings are a rich and integral part of the liturgy of the Church. They have as their basis God's words, they celebrate our faith, and they are signs of the spiritual effects achieved through Jesus' intercession in our daily lives.

The *Book of Blessings* reflects three interrelated realities: blessings are liturgies; they flow from the inspired proclamation of the word of God; they are celebrated by and for those who share in the one priesthood of Christ on behalf of the world.

The *Book of Blessings* presents formularies for all kinds of ministerial blessings, from those for persons, human activities, and various needs and occasions to the blessing of buildings, churches and liturgical objects, devotional articles, and feasts and liturgical times. It also provides instructions to ministers who offer these blessings.

Deacons, by virtue of their ordination, can perform most blessings of the Church. These include people, rosaries and other devotional articles, homes, vehicles, etc. Please note that is not within the scope of this book to review all the blessings contained in the *Book of Blessings*! But most deacons have spent plenty of their time in ministry doing blessings of almost every imaginable variety.

Deacons also should understand that since the ministry of blessing involves a particular exercise of the priesthood of Christ, there is an order to the exercise of this ministry. (Awareness of this "order" helps deacons to avoid misunderstandings during the pastoral application of blessings in parish ministry.)

Therefore, the exercise of the blessing ministry is determined in this manner: It belongs to the Bishop's ministry to preside at diocesan celebrations or those with a large number of faithful attending; it belongs to the priest's ministry to preside at those blessings that involve the community he is appointed to serve; it belongs to the deacon's ministry to preside at those blessings indicated in the *Book of Blessings*, because as minister of the word, liturgy and charity, the deacon is the assistant of the Bishop and the college of presbyters. However, when a priest is present, it is more fitting that the office of presiding is assigned to him; then the deacon assists the priest; a formally instituted acolyte or lector, which are official offices of the Church, is preferred over another layman as the minister of blessings in the absence of a priest or deacon; laymen and women, by virtue of their share in Christ's universal priesthood, may celebrate certain blessings indicated by the book. But they should preside at those blessings only in the absence of a priest or deacon, and relative to their official ministerial responsibilities within the parish. They also must use the special texts designated for lay ministers.

When a deacon presides at the celebration of a blessing, there is a typical structure to the service. It consists of two parts: proclamation of the word of God, and praise of God's goodness and the petition for his help. Usually, rites for beginning and concluding the blessings are proper to the liturgy.

Specific signs of blessing (outstretching, raising or joining of hands, laying on of hands, sprinkling with holy water, incensation, and, particularly, the Sign of the Cross) are indicated by the book; these signs specifically have been mandated to recall God's saving act and to emphasize the relationship between the blessing liturgy and the Church's sacraments. They should always be used according to the norms and rubrics provided.

Deacons should be properly vested in an alb, cincture, and white stole (or a color corresponding to the liturgical time or feast) when presiding at blessings communally, especially those celebrated in a church. (A surplice worn with cassock can replace the alb, cincture, and a cope may be worn for more solemn occasions.)

Finally, note that the book does not contain all blessings. Deacons should look to *Catholic Household Blessings & Prayers*; this is a rich resource for blessings that can be a treasure trove of faith-building for everyday life experiences. All deacons should have one on their reference shelves for parish use.

Devotions

Devotional prayer is a non-liturgical prayer form that promotes an individual's faith. Devotions may be celebrated by a group, but they remain personal prayer. While the Church was rich with devotional prayer before Vatican II, that Council reaffirmed that the practice of devotions "should be highly endorsed, provided they accord with the laws and norms of the Church, above all when they are ordered by the Apostolic See."[26]

While not liturgical prayer, devotions are governed by similar principles of worship. They must be: Trinitarian in nature (mediated by Christ, to the Father in union with the Holy Spirit; ecclesial, as they are integrated with the mission and spirit of the Church; scriptural ("fortified" with readings from Scripture); and often liturgical in origin—associated with the sacraments and reflecting the liturgical calendar.

Deacons may preside at all devotional prayer; the customary vestments for these prayers is alb, cincture, and stole; a cope also may sometimes be worn, depending on the prayer form. Some of the more common devotions include: Stations of the Cross; recitation of the Rosary; blessing of the throats on the feast day of Saint Blaise; distribution of ashes and palms; various novenas and devotions (for example, Chaplet of Divine Mercy, Sacred Heart devotions); May crowning, Forty Hours adoration; blessing of Easter baskets; Saint Francis blessing of the animals; ethnic or culturally inspired celebrations like Our Lady of Guadalupe, Simbang Gabi, and so on.

Finally, one of the more popular Eucharistic devotions these days is Benediction. A deacon is an ordinary minister for the exposition of the Eucharist. He should vest in alb, cincture, and white stole. Also, a deacon should wear a white cope and humeral veil to give the blessing at the end of adoration when using the monstrance; or the humeral veil if the blessing is given with the ciborium.

Benediction may be celebrated at the end of Mass or after Mass (immediately after the distribution of Holy Communion, when the monstrance is placed on the altar), during the Liturgy of the Hours, or during a Eucharistic service. In fact, the ritual book notes "it is appropriate" that Evening Prayer be celebrated in the presence of the Blessed Sacrament.[27]

The deacon with other ministers approaches the altar in silence or while instrumental music is playing. If the Blessed Sacrament is already exposed, the ministers reverence it with a genuflection and go to their chairs. If the Blessed Sacrament is not exposed, the deacon goes directly to the tabernacle, brings it to the altar, and places it in the monstrance. He then places incense in the thurible, kneels, and incenses the Eucharist. A suitable song may be sung at this time; if so, the opening hymn is omitted. After incensation, the deacon goes to his chair. An introduction, Psalmody, reading, homily, responsory, Canticle of Mary, intercessions, and the Lord's Prayer are done.

Benediction follows the Lord's Prayer. The deacon goes to the altar, genuflects, and then kneels. A suitable Eucharistic song is sung while he incenses the Blessed Sacrament. He rises and sings/says a prayer listed in the ritual book. Then the deacon puts on the humeral veil, genuflects, and takes the monstrance. He makes the Sign of the Cross over the people in silence. After the blessing, he places the monstrance back upon the altar. He immediately removes the Blessed Sacrament from the monstrance and places it in the tabernacle. An acclamation, for example, the Divine Praises, or song may be sung or instrumental music might be played during this time. Then the deacon and ministers depart from the sanctuary.

NOTES

1. *Presbyterorum Ordinis*, 5.

2. See *General Instruction of the Roman Missal* (GIRM), 16.

3. GIRM, 78.

4. See *Catechism of the Catholic Church* (CCC), 1324–1325.

5. GIRM, 119b.

6. *Redemptionis Sacramentum*, 125.

7. The *Ordo* (Latin for order) is a liturgical almanac, published annually. You will need to use the *Ordo* that is specific to your diocese or religious community. The Ordo includes an entry for every day of the liturgical year, and includes all the information you need to prepare for the Mass. It tells you the liturgical color of the day, it explains where to find the readings and the presidential prayers, and includes notes about the Liturgy of the Hours. It also includes a variety of options for prayers.

8. GIRM, 174.

9. GIRM, 51.

10. *Sing to the Lord: Music in Divine Worship*, 155.

11. GIRM, 137.

12. National Directory for the Formation, Ministry and Life of Permanent Deacons in the United States, USCCB, 2005, 90.

13. *Rite of Christian Initiation of Adults* (RCIA), 15.

14. *Catechism of the Catholic Church*, 1214, quoting 2 Corinthians 5:17; Galatians 6:15; cf. Romans 6:3–4; Colossians 2:12.

15. *Rite of Baptism for Children* (RBC), 8.3.

16. RBC, 7.2.

17. Ibid., 100.

18. See the RBC, 101.

19. RCIA, 197.

20. RBC, 117.

21. *Rite of Confirmation*, 3.

22. *Rite of Penance*, 2.

23. *Rite of Marriage*, 39.

24. Ibid., 43.

25. *Order of Christian Funerals*, 213.

26. *Sacrosanctum Concilium*, 13.

27. *Order for the Solemn Exposition of the Holy Eucharist*, 37.

Frequently Asked Questions

1. What is the difference between a deacon and a priest?

There are really two questions embedded here—one about identity and another about function. A Roman Catholic deacon, as an ordained member of the clergy, shares, with Bishops and priests, in the hierarchical order of the Sacrament of Holy Orders. However, Bishops and priests are ordained into the *priesthood* of Jesus; deacons are ordained into the *ministry* of Jesus. Therefore, a deacon's sacramental ministry comes about by sharing in the ministry of the Bishop, who ordains him for service to the Church and God's people.

The deacon's title comes from the Greek word, *diakonos*, which means service. While all the Church is called to serve one another, the deacon's ministry or service is at the behest of the Bishop and has a specific triple purpose: service to the word, service to the liturgy, and service to charity. Therefore, upon ordination, a deacon is permanently and publicly configured to Christ the Servant; he shares in the pastoral responsibility of the Bishop to serve all people in the diocese, especially in his ministry of word altar and charity; and he becomes a member of the Order of Deacons, which is an integral part of the clerical structure of the Church, collaborating with priests in serving the needs of the diocese.

In terms of the function of deacons, they are ordained to baptize, witness marriages, assist at Eucharist, and preside at other liturgical functions such as Benediction, Liturgy of the Hours, Vigil for the Deceased, funeral liturgies outside of Mass, and committals. Deacons cannot celebrate Mass (they cannot consecrate the elements), hear confessions, or administer the Sacrament of the Anointing of the Sick. Deacons should refer to *Sacrum diaconatus ordinem*, 21-22.

2. What is the difference between a permanent deacon and a transitional deacon?

In terms of Holy Orders, there is no difference. There is only one diaconate, or Order of Deacons. However, permanent deacons, who may be married prior to ordination, retain that clerical rank (deacon) for life. Transitional deacons never marry since they are moving toward ordination to the priesthood, the next step of the hierarchical ministry of the Church.

3. Do deacons' wives have a special role?

A deacon's wife adds an incredible dimension to his ministry because they are both living and modeling how to witness the faith as a married couple. However, a woman married to a man ordained to the diaconate receives no special status or privilege upon her husband's reception of the Sacrament of Holy Orders. And together they should never be called "deacon couples" since only the husband is ordained. The proper term for a woman married to a deacon is "deacon's wife." That said, many wives of deacons are active lay ministers who perform important service in their parish communities. But their ministry is offered through their individual call by God to service, and not simply because they are married to clerics.

4. Can a deacon remarry if his wife dies?

Essentially, no, although he may petition the Holy See for a dispensation to remarry. These permissions are rarely granted.

5. Why did the Second Vatican Council restore the permanent diaconate?

Especially after the horrors of World War II, the Church felt that a sacramental diaconate could help restore the sense of Christ's presence to the world by being an icon of Christ the Servant—thus, by being a cleric living in the world of the laity, the deacon might become a visible sacramental sign of Christ.

6. Most deacons hold "regular" jobs in the world, so I guess deacons are basically part-time ministers?

Ordination affects a man permanently, and once he is ordained a deacon he is always a "full-time" deacon regardless of what job he performs or where he is at a particular time. In fact, his entire essence changes through ordination. That is why deacons are no longer identified with the title of Mr. but Deacon. Also, "deacon" is *who* they are—not a job description or title.

7. What kind of training or formation do deacons receive?

Both the Vatican and the United States Conference of Catholic Bishops have issued directories that govern the formation, ministry, and life of permanent deacons. Most deacon formation programs require four to six years of study and prayer, are affiliated with the diocese's major seminary (which also forms diocesan priests), and includes, among many other elements, academic classes in ecclesiology, Christology, liturgical theology, sacramental theology; sacramental and liturgical skills (including how to preside at Baptism, witness Marriages, assist at Mass, preside at wake services, funeral liturgies outside Mass, committals); integration of the spirituality of the Church with their own individual spiritual lives; and a sharpening of practical pastoral skills of communication, conflict resolution, collaboration, and other people skills.

8. Are there age limits to formation and/or ordination?

In the United States of America, a man cannot be ordained to the permanent diaconate until 35 years of age. There are various diocesan guidelines about the upper age limits for ordination—which generally ranges from 55 to 65.

9. Do deacons get transferred from parish to parish like priests?

The policy of most dioceses allows deacons to be transferred from parish to parish. Remember a deacon, like Bishops and priests, is ordained for the entire diocese, not just his parish, and should be used to best meet the needs of that diocese.

10. Should a deacon's homily be "different" than a priest's homily?

Regardless of how you answer that question, a good homily breaks open the word of God for the assembly by using all kinds of examples, including daily life experiences. This means family life, workplace, leisure activities—and all that it entails. Just be sure to let your family know if they'll be featured in one of your homilies—before you get to the ambo! Otherwise the ride home after Mass could be really interesting.

Resources

Basic Norms for the Formation of Permanent Deacons/Directory for the Ministry and Life of Permanent Deacons. Rome, Italy: Libreria Editrice Vaticana, 1998.

The joint document from the Vatican's Congregation for Catholic Education and the Congregation for the Clergy was issued in 1998. It provides both norms and guidelines for deacon formation programs, the ministry of deacons, and for those characters and qualities that a deacon should evidence and live.

Brown, Raymond E., ss. *Christ in the Gospels of the Liturgical Year: Expanded Edition with Essays by John R. Donahue, SJ, and Ronald D. Witherup, SS.* Collegeville, Minnesota: Liturgical Press, 2008.

A hermeneutical approach to the person of Jesus revealed in scripture. Its methodology follows the liturgical year.

Ditewig, William T. *The Emerging Diaconate: Servant Leaders in a Servant Church.* Mahwah, New Jersey: Paulist Press, 2009.

An examination of the Second Vatican Council's restoration of the diaconate as a permanent order of ordained ministry. It explores the notion that the diaconate envisioned by Vatican II was never intended to recreate the early diaconate, but rather to authentically update the tradition of diaconal orders.

Ditewig, William T. *101 Questions and Answers on Deacons.* Mahwah, New Jersey: Paulist Press, 2004.

Everything you always wanted to know about the diaconate. Includes questions of deacons' requirements, formation, liturgical and sacramental roles, and place in the parish as they serve their (arch)dioceses by sharing in the Bishops' ministries of the word, liturgy, charity, and justice.

Ditewig, William T. *The Deacon at Mass: A Theological and Pastoral Guide*. Mahwah, New Jersey: Paulist Press, 2007.

A theological and pastoral guide to the words, actions, gestures, and movements that are proper to a deacon assisting at the eucharistic liturgy.

Foley, Edward, CAPUCHIN. *Preaching Basics: A Model and a Method*. Chicago, Illinois: Liturgy Training Publications, 2007.

Homiletics is an art, and the preacher an artist. But it is an art form within liturgy, a conversation with the people of God that relates all that scripture teaches to our everyday experiences. The author describes how anyone can become a better preacher if they remember the basics.

General Instruction of the Roman Missal. Washington, D.C.: United States Conference of Catholic Bishops, 2010.

The norms and rubrics for the celebration of the Eucharist that reflect the liturgical reforms of the Second Vatican Council. This document was revised in 2010 and is included in the third edition of *The Roman Missal*.

International Theological Commission. *From the Diakonia of Christ to the Diakonia of the Apostles*. Chicago, Illinois: Hillenbrand Books, 2003.

An historical and theological survey of the diaconate from the time of the apostles following Vatican II.

Keating, James, editor. *The Deacon Reader*. Mahwah, New Jersey: Paulist Press, 2006.

A collection of essays that provide an overview of the theological, sacramental, pastoral, spiritual, and sociological nature of the diaconate. It also discusses diaconate identity and mission.

Muller, Gerhard Ludwig. *Priesthood and Diaconate: The Recipient of the Sacrament of Holy Orders from the Perspective of Creation Theology and Christology*. San Francisco, California: Ignatius Press, 2002.

An exploration of the Church's understanding of the ministerial priesthood and the diaconate as these relate to Pope John Paul II's apostolic letter, *Ordinatio Sacerdotalis*.

National Directory for the Formation, Ministry, and Life of Permanent Deacons in the United States. Washington, D.C.: United States Conference of Catholic Bishops, 2005.

Addresses both norms and guidelines for deacon formation programs, the ministry of deacons, and for those characters and qualities that a deacon should evidence and live.

Osborne, Kenan B., OFM. *The Permanent Diaconate: Its History and Place in the Sacrament of Orders.* Mahwah, New Jersey: Paulist Press, 2007.

An exploration of the three orders of the Church—diaconate, presbyterate, and episcopate—through the lens of post–Vatican II sacramental and systematic theology.

Turner, Paul. *At the Supper of the Lamb: A Pastoral and Theological Commentary on the Mass.* Chicago, Illinois: Liturgy Training Publications, 2011.

This book walks you through each part of the Mass. Its structure follows the Order of Mass in the third edition of *The Roman Missal* and is an invitation to worship, a call to new intention, and a deeper awareness of the privilege we share to be invited to the supper of the Lamb.

Waznak, Robert P. *An Introduction to the Homily.* Collegeville, Minnesota: Liturgical Press, 1998.

Offering valuable insights regarding the meaning and purpose of the homily within the liturgical traditional of the Roman Catholic Church, this book includes references from normative Church documents, and reflections on theological studies and the lived experiences of preachers.

Wood, Susan K., SCL. *Sacramental Orders.* Collegeville, Minnesota: Liturgical Press, 2000.

This work examines the sacramentality of Episcopal ordination, the identity of the presbyterate, and questions about the diaconate through the context of the 1990 Rite of Ordination.

Glossary

ALB: From the Latin *albus* (white), a long white linen gown-like garment worn under other vestments, and common to all liturgical ministers (priests, deacons, instituted ministers of any rank, and lay ministers) and fastened at the waist by a cincture. The alb is white because it is a reminder of the white garment that clothes the newly baptized. Its use goes back to the sixth century.

ALTAR CLOTH: A long table covering of dignified white material that should be placed on the altar out of reverence for the celebration of Mass.

AMBO: A stationary reading stand in the sanctuary, usually of dignified proportions, from where the word of God is proclaimed. Its use is reserved for scriptural readings, the Responsorial Psalm, and Easter Proclamation. It may also be used for the homily and the Prayer of the Faithful.

AMBRY: A niche or cupboard in a church which houses the sacramental oils: Oil of Catechumens, Oil of the Sick, Sacred Chrism. In many churches, this is located in the baptistry.

AMICE: A rectangular piece of linen cloth worn by a priest or deacon to cover his street clothing at the neck. Originally, the *amicticus* (Latin: cloak) partially covered the head. An amice need not be worn if the alb completely covers the cleric's roman collar or street clothes.

AMPHORA: A large pitcher holding enough holy water to pour over an adult during Baptism.

ASPERGILLUM: A wand-like liturgical instrument used to sprinkle holy water.

BAPTISTRY: The part of a church where the baptismal font is located.

BOAT: The small container, often in the approximate shape of a boat, used to hold incense to place in the thurible.

CATHEDRA: Bishop's chair, which is a sign of his teaching authority in the Church.

CHALICE: The cup, made of precious metals, that holds the consecrated wine at Mass.

CHALICE VEIL: A white veil (or liturgical color of the day) that may cover the chalice and pall prior to the chalice's preparation at the Preparation of the Gifts.

CHASUBLE: The vestment proper to the Priest Celebrant at Mass and at other sacred actions connected with the Mass; it is worn over the alb and stole.

CHRISMATORIES: Glass jars or decanters that hold the sacred oils and are placed in the ambry.

CIBORIUM: A sacred vessel with cover generally used to hold consecrated hosts for the distribution of Holy Communion and to be reserved in the tabernacle.

CINCTURE: A cord, usually white, that belts the alb around the waist.

COLLECT: The prayer that gathers together (collects) the prayers of the assembly near the beginning of Mass.

COPE: An ankle-length cloak that may be worn by priests and deacons at liturgies outside of Mass, including Baptism, Benediction, and the Liturgy of the Hours.

CORPORAL: From Latin (*corpus*: body), a square white linen cloth laid upon the altar cloth at the Preparation of the Gifts; the priest places the chalice, paten, and host upon it.

CREDENCE TABLE: A small table near the altar that holds the chalice, paten, corporal, purificators, water cruet, finger bowl, and towel for the celebration of the Eucharistic Liturgy.

CRUET: Small flask or container that holds water or wine for the celebration of Eucharist. The wine cruet may be replaced with a flagon.

CUSTODIA: A fitted metal case which holds the lunette, which is used for eucharistic exposition.

DALMATIC: The outer liturgical garment proper to the deacon, worn over the alb and stole at Mass and in processions. It often has ample cut sleeves, is usually at least knee length, and follows the liturgical color of the day/season.

EPICLESIS: An invitation of the Holy Spirit to come upon the gifts (and later the people assembled) during the Eucharistic Prayer.

FLAGON: A large container resembling a carafe used to hold wine brought up by the assembly at the Preparation of the Gifts during Mass.

FONT: The receptacle of various shapes and sizes containing water at which Baptisms are performed. Holy water fonts are the small vessels used to hold blessed water. They are usually located near the entrance of a church or chapel.

HUMERAL VEIL: A long, rectangular silk shawl worn over the shoulders by priests and deacons to cover the hands when holding sacred vessels containing the Body of Christ.

LAVABO: A pitcher and bowl used for the washing of the priest's hands during Mass.

LECTERN: A simple podium for the leading of song and making announcements.

LUNETTE: A French term ("little moon") for the small circular glass receptacle which can be inserted into a monstrance for Eucharistic Adoration or devotion; also called a luna or lunula.

MITER: A pointed head cover or hat with two strips of material (called fanons or lappets) worn by Bishops (and abbots) during liturgical celebrations.

MONSTRANCE: A usually ornate vessel, with a round, transparent container, used to view the consecrated host; sometimes called an ostensorium.

NARTHEX: The entrance hall between a church's front doors and its main interior; sometimes called the vestibule or gathering space.

NAVE: The main body of a church, given because of its imagined resemblance to a ship.

ORDO: A book that gives detailed information about each day of the liturgical year, including vestment colors, Lectionary readings, options for prayers, etc.

PALL: A sacred square cloth of white linen lined with cardboard used to place over the chalice at Mass. The term also is used for the large white, cloth covering placed over coffins at funeral Masses.

PASTORAL STAFF: A staff resembling a shepherd's crook carried by the Bishop during liturgical celebrations.

PATEN: A sacred vessel resembling a small, flat plate used to hold the host at Mass.

PURIFICATOR: A small cloth used for wiping the paten and drying the chalice at Mass.

PYX: A small metallic container used by ministers of Communion to hold consecrated hosts; most often used for pastoral care ministries.

SACRARIUM: A special sink within the sacristy for the cleaning of sacred vessels after purification by clerics or instituted ministers. It drains directly into the earth, and not into the sewer system.

SANCTUARY LAMP: A candle or oil lamp lit to indicate the presence of the Eucharist in the tabernacle.

SITULA: The traditional bucket or ornate bowl that holds holy water for various orders of blessings.

STOLE: A narrow strip of cloth worn over both shoulders by priests, and over the left shoulder, diagonally across the chest, and fastened near the hip, by deacons. Most often, it is worn under a chasuble or dalmatic. The stole marks the authority of Bishops, priests, and deacons. There are two types of stoles: sacerdotal and diaconal.

SURPLICE: A waist-length white garment worn over a cassock.

TABERNACLE: The large permanent container resembling a safe that holds the consecrated hosts in a church. It is a place of sacred reservation and prayer.

THURIBLE: A vessel made of metal and hanging from chains that carries hot coals and incense in procession. The minister who tends this vessel is called a thurifer.

VIMPA: A cloth placed around the shoulder of an acolyte or altar server used to hold a miter and crosier of the Bishop.

ZUCHETTO: A colored skull cap worn by Bishops and others: white for pope; red for cardinals; purple for Bishops and Archbishops; black for abbots.

Prayer to the Blessed Virgin Mary

Mary,
Who as teacher of faith, by your obedience to the word of God, has
co-operated in a remarkable way with the work of redemption, make the
ministry of deacons effective by teaching them to hear the Word and to
proclaim it faithfully.

Mary,
Teacher of charity, who by your total openness to God's call, has co-operated
in bringing to birth all the Church's faithful, make the ministry and the life
of deacons fruitful by teaching them to give themselves totally to the service
of the People of God.

Mary,
Teacher of prayer, who through your maternal intercession has supported
and helped the Church from her beginnings, make deacons always attentive
to the needs of the faithful by teaching them to come to know the value
of prayer.

Mary,
Teacher of humility, by constantly knowing yourself to be the servant of the
Lord you were filled with the Holy Spirit, make deacons docile instruments
in Christ's work of redemption by teaching them the greatness of being the
least of all.

Mary,
Teacher of that service which is hidden, who by your everyday and ordinary
life filled with love, knew how to co-operate with the salvific plan of God in
an exemplary fashion, make deacons good and faithful servants, by teaching
them the joy of serving the Church with an ardent love.

Amen.

—Congregation for the Clergy, "Directory for the Ministry and Life of Permanent
Deacons," Appendix.